MW01254926

PIONEERS
OF THE
POSSIBLE

Celebrating Visionary Women of the World

This book is dedicated to all the inspiring women in and beyond these pages.
As you live a life that honors who you are, you encourage every woman
to make the same journey for herself.

❝ The goal of life is to make your heartbeat match the beat of the universe, to match your nature with Nature. ❞

Joseph Campbell

Text © 2012 Angella M. Nazarian.
Cover portrait of Frida Kahlo © Rue des Archives/AGIP.
Endpages designed and illustrated by Camille Dubois.
© 2012 Assouline Publishing
601 West 26th Street, 18th Floor
New York, NY 10001, USA
www.assouline.com
ISBN: 978-1-61428-039-2
Color separation by Spectragraphic.
Printed in China by Hing Yip Printing Co., Ltd.

ANGELLA M. NAZARIAN

PIONEERS
OF THE
POSSIBLE

Celebrating Visionary Women of the World

ASSOULINE

Contents

Portrait of the author by Brian Morri.

Introduction

Today, perhaps more than any other time in modern history, women feel empowered to follow their true callings. For the past six years, I have been part of a small group of Los Angeles women that gathers regularly to share ideas, hopes, and fears, and also to look out for one another as we pass through the various stages of our lives. These friends come from all walks of life, and we are unified by the shared experience of womanhood.

Our discussions often center on creating lives of meaning that will leave us fulfilled and uplifted. And we're always looking for examples of women who got it right. We share anecdotes about inspiring women and try to glean what we can from their approaches to life. What did Sandra Day O'Connor do "just right" that landed her on the United States Supreme Court? How did Oprah Winfrey, Indra Nooyi, Tina Brown, and Martha Stewart achieve such platinum success with so few female role models before them? And tough women like Hillary Rodham Clinton, Madeleine Albright, and Arianna Huffington have a more difficult job navigating the political waters than like-minded men; what have these women got that gives them the edge?

As I drove home from one of these gatherings not long ago, an idea popped into my head: What if I created a fantasy party and invited women whose stories had moved me? Who would I invite?

This silly idea—the kind you think about while driving but never share with anyone—actually stayed with me for a while. And after a few weeks, it morphed. I started collecting names, and my little project took on a spirit of its own. And that's how this book came to be. Eventually, I whittled down my long list to twenty remarkable souls who represent the wide and wonderful world of women.

What a group of pioneers! The collection includes a business tycoon and an author, a dancer and a philosopher, a spiritual leader, a social activist—and even a bullfighter. Many are also wives and mothers. Each has her own special way of expressing her spirit—whether through painting, politics, environmentalism, architecture, or athletics. Every one imagined what did not yet exist—but might someday. That's why I call them Pioneers of the Possible. They are all optimists, and their lives are filled with a delicious passion.

As I read about these trailblazing women, sifting through volumes of biographies, memoirs, and news clippings, I began to feel a special bond with each of them. I pinned their pictures on my office wall. I found myself thinking of them often. Yes, these women became my new friends—special friends whose life perspectives inspired me deeply.

Although they may not have been born on the same continent or even during the same time period, these women are all part of a continuous chain linking one person, one place, or one event to the next.

While researching the life of the author Anaïs Nin, for example, I was surprised to discover that the critical thinker Simone de Beauvoir occupied the same Parisian house that she did—only decades later. While studying the American sculptor Isamu Noguchi's long-lasting friendship and collaboration with the modern dance legend Martha Graham, I found that he also carried on a torrid love affair with the exceptional painter Frida Kahlo. In examining Somaly Mam's humanitarian work in the field of human sex trafficking, I learned that this courageous Cambodian woman shared the same stage with the Guatemalan activist Rigoberta Menchú Tum when they both received the prestigious Prince of Asturias Award for International Cooperation in 1998. And these coincidences, interwoven like threads in a colorful quilt, continued throughout the project.

I discovered, too, that these women shared some critical characteristics. As leadership expert Marcus Buckingham discerned in researching his best-selling 2009 book, *Find Your Strongest Life—What the Happiest and Most Successful Women Do Differently*: "Study the happiest and most successful women and you realize that they ignore balance, and strive for fullness instead."

Indeed, these visionary women's paths all began with a deep-seated yearning to lead a life brimming with vibrancy. As Anaïs Nin wrote: "I am possessed by a fever for knowledge, experience, and creation" and "I only believe in fire. Life. Fire. Being myself on fire, I set others on fire." Surely her passion-filled life has sparked the imagination of many women today. Forugh Farrokhzad's quest was similar; she searched for a path to bring her closer to a numinous state—the rapture of being fully alive and creating. No wonder she became the most lauded female poet in Iranian history!

As my women's discussion group has discovered, our enthusiasm for life seems to be quietly sustained from somewhere within us, wedded to our own particular inclinations. The key to success for many of the pioneers showcased here is that they are in tune with their own emotional reactions to specific life moments. They act as if they are on a personal journey to discover the source of their deepest bliss. Once they find it, they dedicate themselves to its ongoing pursuit.

Certainly many of these women didn't have an early inkling of what they wanted to do with their lives. The First Lady of Jazz, Ella Fitzgerald, practically stumbled into her career when, as a teenager, she changed her focus from dancing to singing at the last minute for an amateur contest at the Apollo Theater. The entrepreneur Jacqueline Novogratz was a successful banker before a revelatory personal experience prompted her to explore a new career—as a philanthropist. Today, through her innovative Acumen Fund, she's changing the face of global philanthropy.

The groundbreaking dancer-choreographer Martha Graham once said: "You have to keep open and aware directly to the urges that motivate you… There is a vitality, a life force, an energy, a quickening that is translated through you into action, and because there is only one of you in all of time, this expression is unique. And if you block it, it will never exist through any other medium and be lost."

I firmly believe that every single one of us has something special to do in this world. Given our uniqueness, it's not surprising that one of our greatest challenges is to fully inhabit our own individuality—to discover which path best expresses who we are and what connects us to our passions. Who would have thought that a poor Indian woman with a fervent spiritual inclination to embrace and love would one day become Mata Amritanandamayi, known as Amma, the Hugging Saint of India, an internationally renowned spiritual leader. Or consider the life of Conchita Cintrón, the most respected female bullfighter in history: This was, to be sure, not a common profession for a woman to gravitate toward in the late 1930s and '40s. Similarly, Gertrude Berg broke all boundaries by becoming the first woman to create a media empire and launch the first television sitcom—ever—in America. For all these women, the key to a fulfilling life was a willingness to embrace what was unique to them.

Each identified her personal source of genius, then built a life—and a career—around it. No doubt, honoring and making use of our strengths pays larger dividends than concentrating on our perceived weaknesses. Estée Lauder, the woman behind the wildly successful cosmetic brand, had a mantra: "Be large enough to admit any possibility… make the most of what you have." The Mexican artist Frida Kahlo honored herself and her heritage in intense, brilliantly colored, primitivistic self-portraits and became a world famous painter. The French writer Simone de

Beauvoir used her remarkable intellectual skills to become one of the twentieth century's most celebrated philosophers and feminist icons.

Even when these women aligned their work with their soul-driven passions, many were still forced to overcome obstacles. Helen Suzman, the longtime South African legislator and antiapartheid activist, had to fight through decades of opposition before she witnessed true freedom for her country's nonwhite majority. Marina Silva, the environmentalist and politician who ultimately ran for president of Brazil, was illiterate and lived in the Amazon rain forest until the age of sixteen.

The theme of resilience comes up with great frequency in my women's group. Of course, our setbacks are quite different—the loss of a job, the loss of a husband, even the loss of spirit. But the challenge to learn is the same. "How do I move forward?" we ask.

From the inspiring life of Wangari Maathai, the Kenyan politician and environmental activist who won the 2004 Noble Peace Prize, we learn the value of resilience: "Every person who has ever achieved anything has been knocked down many times. But all of them picked themselves up and kept going, and that is what I have always tried to do," she said. Somaly Mam, the human rights advocate, has saved thousands of young women who were locked into sexual slavery. Once a sex-trafficking victim herself, she risks her life on a daily basis to rescue and rehabilitate others. And surely the dramatic life of the 1992 Nobel Peace Prize winner, Rigoberta Menchú Tum, the Guatemalan human rights activist who lost many family members in her fight for justice, is the embodiment of the indomitable spirit. Setbacks for these women were temporary; they all found ways to overcome even the most daunting obstacles.

Often, self-doubt forces us into lives that are too small for our dreams. But having studied this group of hyper-achievers, I learned that self-doubt had no place in their DNA. When we doubt ourselves, we must find a path back to our strength. Consider the example of Dharma Master Cheng Yen, known as the Mother Teresa of the Far East. "Never underestimate the power of smallness," she has said. She was a Buddhist nun with just a primary school education living in a poor, remote area of Taiwan with five disciples, yet she dreamed of building hospitals and helping the needy all over the world. Today, her Tzu Chi Foundation has ten million members worldwide. "When the time comes, I will know exactly what to do," she said, showing that faith in our own abilities is invaluable in combating self-doubt.

We can learn too from the highly motivated female athlete. Sometimes, combining faith, physical ability, and discipline can take us very far. It took Nawal El Moutawakel from the streets of Casablanca to the Olympic arena: In 1984, she became the first African-born Muslim woman to earn an Olympic gold medal.

Perhaps the most important characteristic shared by all visionary leaders is the courage to make that leap of faith at every critical crossroad. "Life shrinks and expands in proportion to one's courage," Anaïs Nin wisely said. Some think courage means fearlessness. But Jacqueline Novogratz has a different perspective: "It is not that good leaders are fearless, but that they see possibility where others don't." It is with this very spirit that the Pritzker Prize–winning Iraqi-born architect Zaha Hadid has forged her remarkably successful career. Early clients sometimes looked at her deconstructivist, fantasy-like plans and declared them too radical to be built. But her ever-growing list of global commissions has proved otherwise. Visionaries have the courage to act on a dream. As Zaha puts it: "Believe in the impossible."

"Trust yourself," said Israel's courageous Golda Meir, the third woman in the world to become a prime minister. "Create the kind of self that you will be happy to live with all your life. Make the most of yourself by fanning the tiny, inner sparks of possibility into flames of achievement."

Our purpose in life may impact something as large as a nation or as small as our immediate community. In most cases, it is multilayered. But no matter where we are headed, learning about the lives of pioneering women is an inspiring way to honor who we are and to encourage each other toward greater possibilities and deeper lives.

I truly hope that these twenty profiles ignite you to shine your own unique light—fully and wholeheartedly. Researching and writing them certainly did that for me.

Angella M. Nazarian

66 One is not born a woman
—one becomes one. 99

Simone de Beauvoir

66 A seed is like a little girl: It can
look small and worthless, but if you
treat it well then it will grow beautiful. 99

Somaly Mam

66 You are unique, and if that
is not fulfilled, then something
has been lost. 99

Martha Graham

66 And when I'm by myself
sometimes I wonder—did I really
become the woman I wanted
to be—or am I still trying? 99

Gertrude Berg

" I believe in the impossible. "

Zaha Hadid

" Feet, why do I need them if I have wings to fly? "

Frida Kahlo

" I've learned that there is no currency like trust and no catalyst like hope. "

Jacqueline Novogratz

" The future... belongs to the feminine. "

Nawal El Moutawakel

Mata
AMRITANANDAMAYI
"AMMA"

(1953–)

The Divine Mother

Posted banners seemed to cover Wilshire Boulevard. On every one, an Indian woman stood in a white sari, laughing. Below her were the dates for the Los Angeles leg of her world tour, along with a name: Amma. Driving by them for what seemed like the umpteenth time that week, I thought to myself, *Who is Amma?*

That very day, I mentioned the banners to a friend over lunch. "Amma is the 'Hugging Saint,'" she explained, "and she travels the world giving hugs to hundreds of thousands of people a year." I leaned across the table, baffled. "You mean thousands of people wait in line to get a hug from her?" My friend continued stirring her cappuccino, smiling and nodding her head.

Curiosity got the better of me, and ten days later I found myself seated, along with three thousand others, in the ballroom of a cavernous Los Angeles International Airport hotel. Scanning the room, no particular profile or demographic stood out. A computer engineering professor sat to my left, a German mother and baby were on my right, and a young cancer patient sat in front. As the day progressed, more people streamed in and sat at the end of the line.

Before Amma took the stage, a group of musicians played traditional Hindu devotional music. Then the lights went dark, and we watched a short film depicting the extensive humanitarian work that Amma has inspired and started across the globe. Her nonprofit organization, Mata Amritanandamayi Math, has provided development assistance, medical aid, economic aid, and educational facilities to the world's neediest. More than two million poor people are fed each year through various centers; more than forty thousand houses have been built for the homeless across India; and nearly $46 million has been donated for tsunami relief. M. A. Math also builds elderly care centers, orphanages, schools, and hospitals in India and has established programs designed to eradicate leprosy, AIDS, and tuberculosis. And the list goes on and on.

As the lights went up, Amma took her seat in the center of the stage. Her sari-clad devotees began directing the audience to approach her one by one. I witnessed more than eight hundred hugs before my turn came, and what I saw touched me deeply. While being held, some smiled, some broke down and cried, and others just peered deeply into her eyes.

It is hard to fathom that since the mid-seventies, Amma has received people every day for hugs, embracing more than twenty-five million human beings throughout the world. In one day alone, she has been known to hug for more than twenty hours straight, wrapping her arms around as many as fifty thousand people.

> If we adopt the spiritual principles in our life, then no matter what situations we have to face, we will be able to deal with them in a positive way. We will develop the strength to overcome any ordeal.

Amma, whose name means simply "Mother," is revered as a living saint and a sage by millions in India. She has dedicated herself to manifesting unconditional love and compassion—qualities that Hindus attribute to the Divine Mother, or the feminine aspect of God. Amma has said, "The beauty and charm of selfless love and service should not die away from the face of the earth. The world should know that a life of dedication is possible, that a life inspired by love and service to humanity is possible."

While waiting my turn, I wondered if it would be awkward to be held by someone I'd never met. When I approached her, she wrapped her arms around me and held me tight. She hummed in my ear, and then, within seconds, stopped and whispered these words in my native language of Persian: "You are good enough the way you are." She then released me and handed me a Hershey's Kiss. (Apparently no one leaves her company without a small gift.)

Did I find it awkward to be in her arms? The answer is an unequivocal no. Several other feelings washed over me, though. Cradled in her pillow-like bosom, I had this strange, familiar sensation of being enveloped by mothers of past generations. I was curious to know how she had recognized that I was Persian, and was dumbfounded that she had spoken in my native tongue. I was surprised by what she had whispered. But the overwhelming feeling streaming through me was that of connectivity. Truthfully, I can't say it was the hug itself that I found so transformative; it was the space that Amma had created for so many. Just imagine how it must feel to be among fifty thousand people who have gathered simply to experience unconditional love!

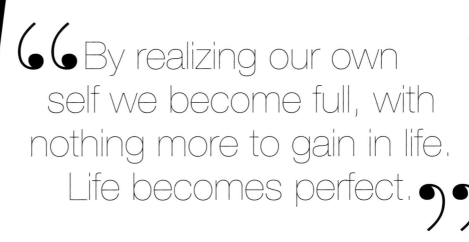

"By realizing our own self we become full, with nothing more to gain in life. Life becomes perfect."

Previous pages: Amma in Pontoise, France, during her European tour, October 2009. *From top left:* Amma on her European tour, 2009; a collage of Amma portraits, 2008; Amma and followers at the New York stop of Amma's U.S. tour, 2005; Amma hugs a disciple during her 2002 U.S. tour.

So how did this extraordinary woman and spiritual icon come to be?

Sudhamani (Amma's birth name) was born in September 1953 in a small, poor fishing village in the state of Kerala in southwestern India. For generations, Amma's father's family lived in the village on a narrow island full of coconut and banana trees and fished the clear waters of the Arabian Sea. Her mother, Damayanti, recalls that the birth of her third child was an easy one—she felt almost no pain. But after delivery, her baby's face was dark blue, and the infant was utterly silent, so Damayanti thought she'd had a stillbirth. Thankfully, though, the baby soon took her first breaths, and her blue skin became a dark brown.

As has happened in many cultures that have been influenced by foreign standards, in India a darker complexion was thought to be inferior to a lighter one. So from the start, Amma—who was darker than her two siblings—was treated very poorly. Things took a turn for the worse when her parents noticed that their young daughter was praying incessantly and fervently to Krishna, the most popular Hindu god. Her constant chanting and emotional displays alarmed her parents. In a determined effort to make her into a "normal" child, they beat her regularly and treated her cruelly.

According to Judith Cornell's biography, *Amma: Healing the Heart of the World*, young Amma was pulled out of school for good during the fourth grade to help her ailing mother with the housework. With Amma at home, her parents became even more exasperated by her behavior. She began embracing the destitute, formerly known as Dalits, or "untouchables," who passed by their house, bringing them extra food and eating with them. Despite the harsh physical abuse she experienced at the hands of her parents as a result, Amma persisted.

At thirteen, her parents sent her off to be an indentured servant for various family members. But Amma quarreled so much that she was sent home. To the dismay of her parents, her strange behavior continued, prompting them to question her mental faculties. She hugged trees and animals and kissed plants and children. She spent a good part of every night dancing in a state of ecstasy, losing track of time.

To rid themselves of their awkward child, her parents decided to marry her off quickly. However, Amma put an abrupt end to her parents' scheme by running into the living room where her young suitor was waiting, screaming, and waving a pestle like a weapon. Needless to say, the terrified young man ran out of the house and never came back.

By the time she was twenty-one, Amma had developed a following. She had chosen a small banyan tree under which she would dance, pray, and hug those who came to her. Hugging was the most natural and maternal way for Amma to bless those who visited her. She mixed freely with all kinds of people, regardless of age, gender, or caste—a practice deemed scandalous for a young Indian woman at that time. But she was steadfast in her determination to embody the loving and compassionate energy of the Divine Mother. "We don't know who you are," her distressed father pleaded. "Perhaps you are divine. But we are ordinary people. Let Divine Mother rest in heaven, and behave like a normal girl."

Amma ignored her parents' pleas. In fact, according to Cornell, she audaciously predicted, "In time, this place will become a spiritual center. Many of my devotees will flock here from far and wide, and some will settle here. I myself will travel around the world, many times."

And, sure enough, by 1979, a group had begun to organize around Amma. By 1981, the first ashram was established in her village in Kerala. Today, that ashram is just one of thirty-three centers around the world. Amma began traveling in 1987 and now enjoys an annual world tour. The first ashram has become a six-story temple surrounded by residential buildings. At 4:30 a.m. each morning, just as all the Hindu temples down the coast begin to blare their sacred chants through loudspeakers, the residents of Amma's ashram prepare for their daily meditation, to be followed by several hours of service. Amma's devotees across the vast continent of India number in the millions, and some seven thousand people show up three evenings a week at the original Amritapuri Ashram to receive her blessings.

If we penetrate deeply into all aspects and all areas of life, we will find that hidden behind everything is love. We will discover that love is the force, the power, and inspiration behind every word and every action.

Today, her parents no longer see her as their inferior, dark-skinned daughter. They honor her as a great saint. "This transformation in Amma's parents is perhaps her greatest miracle. But it was a slow, evolutionary process that took many years," says Swami Amritaswarupananda, Amma's first disciple and the vice chairman of M. A. Math.

Amma's stature as a spiritual leader is particularly unique in India, where men traditionally hold such esteemed positions. Her generous spirit of service and love, coupled with Mahatma Gandhi's conviction that women are intellectually and spiritually equal to men, has certainly helped reshape some expectations of traditional Indian gender roles. "I have put all my hopes in women. I strongly feel that the ultimate victory of nonviolence depends wholly on women," said Gandhi. "They are bound to succeed in whatever they undertake."

Amma has expounded on Gandhi's wise words by helping to support women's rights and causes. Through her nonprofit trust, penniless widows receive pensions and free housing. She encourages married Indian women to become educated so that they are able to support themselves. And Amma has singlehandedly initiated the movement to have women take part in priestly rituals.

Amma's reputation has earned her considerable global reach. She was named one of three presidents to represent the Hindu faith by the 1993 Parliament of the World's Religions. In 1995, Amma gave a keynote speech, "Unity Is Peace," at the Cathedral of Saint John the Divine, in New York City, as part of the interfaith celebrations of the fiftieth-anniversary summit of the United Nations. Kofi Annan, the former secretary-general of the U.N., invited Amma to speak at the U.N. Millennium World Peace Summit in August of 2000—an unprecedented event at which one thousand religious leaders of different faiths came together to forge a partnership of peace. True to her personal and spiritual philosophy, Amma condemned terrorism and violence in the name of religion: "Love is the only medicine that can heal the wounds of the world," she proclaimed. "Where love exists, there cannot be conflict of any kind; peace alone will reign." And it comes as no surprise that she was awarded the 2002 Gandhi-King Award for Non-Violence in recognition of her lifelong work in furthering the principles of peace.

Despite being one of India's most illustrious sages, Amma does not personally claim to be a saint or an incarnation of God. She has no interest in converting people, either. She notes that all religions share the same underlying truth, and no one religion is better than another. As Sister Rose Mercurio, a respected minister in St. Louis, has eloquently said, "Amma affirms in me what I believe—that there is a God in each of us, longing to touch the God in everyone else." Such is the nature of her relationships with other spiritual leaders. The Tibetan monk Lobsang Dorjee Rinpoche and Monsignor Vigile, the bishop of the French Orthodox Church, are among many prominent contemporary spiritual luminaries who claim that their interfaith dialogue with Amma is about finding the common language of the heart.

So why is it that Amma draws crowds of thousands to hear—and feel—her message of love and peace all over the globe? New York City, as Guy Trebay wrote in a *Village Voice* article about one of Amma's visits, is "a tough market for prophets" and "not an easy town for seekers, either." And yet more than eight thousand people flocked to her arms on the first two days of a three-day visit in 2008. Simply put, Amma doesn't ask us to renounce our religious affiliations, relationships, or possessions; she only wants to pass on her message of unconditional motherly love.

As simple as that sounds, it is a serious matter. Certainly, a mother's love is one of the most numinous and primal of relationships. The act of beholding—of being taken into our mother's arms—is one of the first sensations most of us experience in life. Psychologists believe that this union between mother and child unconsciously informs the infant of the pure goodness and worth of his or her being, of safety in the world, and of the great power in connection. By being held, we intrinsically understand that our presence in the world is appreciated and reciprocal, and that it is by the mutuality of a loving and supportive relationship that we transform and blossom. On a spiritual level, Amma serves as a reminder and a symbol of that essential bond.

Amma believes that the purpose of one's life is to realize who we really are. "By realizing our own self we become full, with nothing more to gain in life. Life becomes perfect," Amma says. In light of this, I now understand her whispered "You are good enough" as she held me. She wants all who seek her embrace to know that we are good enough—and deserving of love and happiness.

" What people really need
is love and mental healing.
If we have the right mental
attitude, our external
circumstances will change
for the better; then we'll have
both a peaceful mind and
a healthy body. Spirituality is
the principle that teaches us
to 'air-condition' our minds.
Trying to correct our external
circumstances is like trying to
air-condition the whole world.
It cannot be done. "

Amma

Martha
GRAHAM

(1894–1991)

Modern Dancer and Choreographer,
"Acrobat of God"

Most of us can remember standing sheepishly in front of our scolding parents at one time or another. I remember my father's words clearly: "I can tell you are hiding something; it is written all over your face." For most people, this was a warning not to fib or misbehave. But for the young Martha Graham, who went on to become one of the twentieth century's greatest American dancer-choreographers, this lesson would ultimately play an integral part in her creation of an entirely new lexicon.

"You see, no matter what you say, you reveal yourself—you make fists you think I don't notice, your back gets very straight… your eyelids drop. Remember, Martha, movement never lies," her father once told her, as Russell Freedman relates in *Martha Graham: A Dancer's Life*. These wise words rang true for the rest of her life. Her passion was dance and her dream was to create performances that audiences could viscerally feel. Martha knew it was not just the hand and arm gestures that convey feeling. She understood that changes in breathing—a gasp, a sigh, or a laugh—also release emotion. She perfected a technique to contract and release the torso muscles to control the flow of breath during dance. The results were exciting. Audiences all over the world were captivated by the sheer intensity of her performances, and Martha established herself as one of the great creative geniuses of our time.

> There is a vitality, a life force, an energy,
> a quickening that is translated through you into
> action and because there is only one of you
> in all of time, this expression is unique.
> And if you block it, it will never exist through
> any other medium and be lost.

While I've respected Martha Graham for many years, during the past two years her legacy has become even more meaningful to me. Twice a week, I come upon her framed quotation in the dance studio where I take flamenco lessons—"Discipline sets you free"—an inspiring line I hold near and dear as I continue to negotiate the language of dance for myself (though, admittedly, I've yet to master much discipline or freedom in my classes).

Throughout her illustrious, more than seventy-year career as a dancer and a choreographer, Martha studied movement with a passion and constantly sought new sources of inspiration to inform her work. And she found it in some unlikely places. For example, she sat for hours on a bench across from the lion's cage at New York's Central Park Zoo, studying the animal's form and movement, his pace, and the shifting of his weight. She wanted to replicate the purity of movement she found in nature.

She was also influenced by the triumphs of the twentieth century's art, music, and architecture and extracted the essence of these creative disciplines to incorporate into her dances—a revolution at the time. One artist in particular—Wassily Kandinsky—opened her mind to the possibility of artistic overlap. She first set eyes on an abstract painting by Kandinsky at the Art Institute of Chicago, and she was especially taken with a bold slash of red running across a field of blue. Her heart raced at its minimal beauty, its elegant sense of movement. As Freedman recounts: "I nearly fainted because at that moment I knew I was not mad, that others saw the world, saw art, the way I did," she said. Standing before Kandinsky's painting, she promised herself: "I will do that someday. I will make a dance like that."

Martha's vision of her art form—which she called "contemporary dance"—stripped away fanciful flourishes and celebrated spare, minimal movements. The stark costumes and simple makeup she chose for her early work—for example, dancers' faces painted white with a dramatic slash of red at the mouth—echoed that sentiment.

She also pioneered a completely new approach to the relationship between music and dance. In 1928, Louis Horst, her longtime collaborator, musical director, and lover, composed original music to accompany her already-choreographed piece *Fragments*. It is the first music known in America that was written specifically for a dance. In time, Martha went on to collaborate with several other prominent contemporary composers, including Aaron Copland, Samuel Barber, and Gian Carlo Menotti, each of whom composed original music inspired by and penned to match her performances. Notably, Copland's musical score for Graham's most groundbreaking and best-known work, 1944's *Appalachian Spring*, earned him a Pulitzer Prize.

Her dedication to simplicity and purity extended to set design and architecture, and the results were like nothing American audiences had seen before: In her first collaborations with the famed American sculptor Isamu Noguchi, for example, she used his minimal artworks as backdrops on her set, sparking an aesthetic revolution.

The pair's first collaboration took place in 1935 on *Frontier*, which became Martha's trademark and most popular solo. The dance celebrates the American pioneering spirit. Noguchi installed two horizontal poles at the center of the stage to suggest the wooden bars of a rail fence at a frontier outpost. Two ropes stretched upward and outward from behind the fence to symbolize the boundless plains of the American West. Noguchi and Martha's collaborations continued for more than fifty years.

Understandably, one might assume that a woman with such a brilliant career must have known early on that she wanted to be a dancer. But Martha's story did not follow the typical dancer's career trajectory. Martha Graham was born on May 11, 1894, in Allegheny County, Pennsylvania, the daughter of a physician. Her family spent some time in the South before settling in 1909 in Santa Barbara, California. Her upbringing was strict. In the proper Graham household, dancing was not considered an appropriate career choice for a young woman. In fact, Martha did not see her first professional dance performance until she was almost seventeen. But when she did, she fell instantly in love. Mesmerized by the great Ruth St. Denis—and despite the fact that she was just turning seventeen, an unheard of age to seriously begin dancing—she realized she had found her true calling.

The body says what words cannot.

She worked up the courage to tell her parents that she was not going to Vassar, as was expected of her. Instead, she preferred to attend the Cumnock School of Expression, in Los Angeles, an experimental junior college where students studied both academics and theater arts. After her graduation, she went off to join Ruth St. Denis's newly opened dance school in Los Angeles, Denishawn. At the age of twenty-two, when Martha would likely have been considered too old, too short (five feet two), and too ordinary looking to become a professional dancer, (and with little dance training to boot) she set her sights on joining St. Denis's highly acclaimed troupe. Martha's sheer will propelled her onward: She did join the group, although St. Denis was unimpressed and asked her younger partner and husband, Ted Shawn, to take Martha into his class because she didn't "know what to do with her," as Freedman notes.

In her essay "I Am a Dancer," Martha wrote, "We learn by practice. Whether it means to learn to dance by practicing dancing or to learn to live by practicing living, the principles are the same. . . .One becomes in some area an athlete of God." Practice became Martha's life. During the day, she sat intently in the advanced-level class and mentally registered every movement. By night, she would go to the studio alone and practice by herself for hours.

It was an astonishing feat. By 1921, she went on frequent cross-country tours as a featured soloist with America's foremost dance company. She was consumed by her art, and her performances—intensely passionate experiences bordering on the religious—drew attention.

As she said in 1959's *Martha Graham: Dance On Film*, "A dancer's life is the handling of the material of the self so that you are able to hold the stage in full maturity and power where the magical place demands."

Onstage, Martha magically transformed before everyone's eyes and commanded attention. Her deep-set eyes flashed like bolts of lightning; her jet-black hair framed a face that was riveting in its dramatic intensity and aliveness; her body was taut and electric.

Over the years, I have learned that there is no single path to fulfillment for women: Some may find it through family, others through work, while still others are called to serve their communities. Similarly, there is no one formula for happiness. We are all unique in our needs and our modes of expression. The great Martha Graham carved out her own personal and passion-filled road to fulfillment.

> We learn by practice. Whether it means
> to learn to dance by practicing dancing
> or to learn to live by practicing living,
> the principles are the same.

"There is a vitality, a life force, an energy, a quickening that is translated through you into action, and because there is only one of you in all of time, this expression is unique," she once said. "And if you block it, it will never exist through any other medium and be lost." Once she'd found her calling, nothing could stop Martha from dancing through her life.

For more than seventy years, Martha danced, choreographed, and taught with the ideal of sharing her deeply held feelings through the dynamic language of movement. She announced her retirement as a dancer in 1970 but continued to teach and choreograph until the last year of her life. She founded a school that has trained generations of dancers. Today, dance companies all over the world practice the Graham technique. The Martha Graham Dance Company is the oldest continuously performing modern dance troupe in the world.

At an age when most people are ready to hang up their hats and retire, Martha stayed connected to what made her feel most alive—her dancing. She rejected the idea that age depletes one's creative energy and dynamism. Although she struggled with a bout of depression in her seventies, she reemerged with renewed strength and optimism and continued working until the age of ninety-seven. She created a staggering 181 original dances during her long career and embarked on lengthy tours around the world with her dancers into her eighties and nineties. In her last decade, she created a dozen new works, her most joyful being the one she composed at age ninety-six, *Maple Leaf Rag*.

At ninety-six, she was still what she called an athlete of God, a passionate and undeniably magnetic presence. She danced and danced her way through life—to the very end. As Freedman notes, "When the curtains rose [after the show] she would be seen standing there, proud and erect, wrapped in a shimmering Halston gown, glowing," illuminating her great and contagious joy for life.

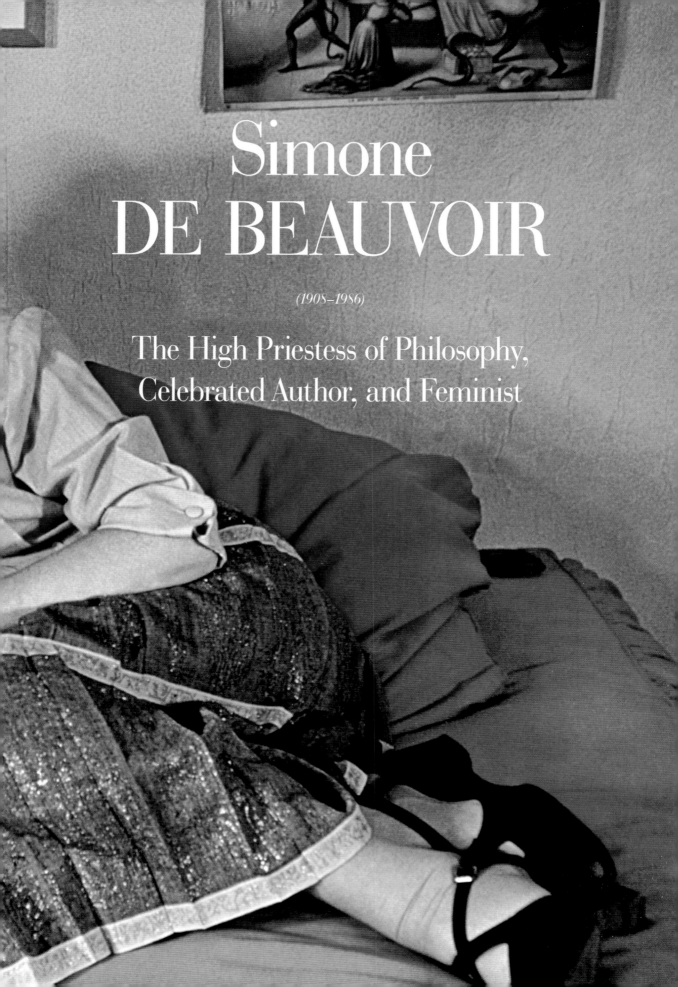

Simone
DE BEAUVOIR

(1908–1986)

The High Priestess of Philosophy, Celebrated Author, and Feminist

For generations, the famed Seine River has sliced Paris into two distinct sections—the Left Bank and the Right Bank. And while the differences between the two districts have narrowed over the years, almost everyone, it seems, whether tourist or resident, still maintains a clear-cut affinity for one or the other: The Right Bank is a bastion of old money, with picturesque, orderly streets, and time-honored grand restaurants; the Left Bank offers romantic, narrow streets, buzzing sidewalk cafés, and an artsy, bohemian vibe.

Having spent time on both sides, I consider myself a Left Bank convert. While I still love the beauty and tradition of the Right, I'm drawn to the old haunts of iconic creative souls like Pablo Picasso, Henri Matisse, and Alberto Giacometti, who spent their days smoking, drinking, thinking, talking, and painting along Saint-Germain-des-Prés. Sipping hot chocolate at the perennially popular Café de Flore, skimming *Le Monde*, and eavesdropping on modern-day café society, I wonder about my favorite existentialist philosopher, Simone de Beauvoir. Was she ever seated at my table?

Live with no time out.

Simone's story reflects the historical tensions between the values of the Right and Left Banks. Born into an upper-crust world, she seemed destined for a life of privilege, poised to embrace the traditions of the Right. But she set her sights on a more free-spirited path, making a decision to live a life devoted to literature and philosophy, with passion and conviction. A legendary mind, a pen, and paper were her weapons, and with them she expressed ideas that changed the way women defined themselves in many parts of the world.

But with few, if any, role models to pattern herself after, how did a young, Catholic, dutiful daughter, bound by classic bourgeois social conventions, find the courage to become the indomitable, outspoken Marxist intellectual who was regarded by French feminists as "the spiritual mother of the young generation"?

Simone grew up in a large apartment at 103, boulevard du Montparnasse in Paris with full-time help and fashionable furnishings. Her father, Georges, lavished attention on his first-born daughter, encouraging her intellectual precociousness. He proudly declared that she "has a man's brain; she thinks like a man," and treated her as if she were an educational equal and an adult. Despite her talents and intelligence, though, both her parents believed Simone's future happiness depended mostly on a "good marriage."

As a young woman, she considered marrying her cousin Jacques Champigneulle. But too many differences marked their relationship. "He accepts luxury and easy living; he likes being happy. But I want my life to be an all-consuming passion. I need to act, to give freely of myself, to bring plans to fruition: I need an object in life, I want to overcome difficulties and succeed in writing a book," she wrote in her diary. "I could never be satisfied with the things that satisfy him." This, it seems, became her life's manifesto.

By the time Simone reached age nineteen, much had changed in the de Beauvoir household: Most of the family fortune was lost just after World War I. The family moved to a smaller apartment and let go of the household staff. Françoise, Simone's mother, worked hard to keep up appearances, but the family struggled to stay afloat and food was often rationed.

"You girls will never marry," Georges repeatedly told Simone and her younger sister, Hélène. "You have no dowries." These words stuck with Simone, and she carried the emotions and memories of her sudden impoverishment into her adult years. Throughout the rest of her life, she decoded childhood incidents in various situations, whether through her writings or through her relationships with various men and women.

> I have been aware of my shortcomings and my limits,
> but I have made the best of them. When I was tormented
> by what was happening in the world, it was the world
> I wanted to change, not my place in it.

But her father's words also served as a catalyst for Simone's success. "You girls must study hard to prepare yourselves to work all your lives," he warned, according to Deirdre Bair's definitive 1991 *Simone de Beauvoir: A Biography*. If his daughters were to enter the workplace, Georges wanted the best for them.

Simone heeded her father's advice. Her destination—after studying mathematics at the Institut Catholique de Paris and literature and language at the Institut Sainte-Marie—turned out to be the Sorbonne, where she focused on philosophy. She finished in a mere three years—a spectacular feat. Then, in 1929, at age twenty-one, Simone became the youngest student ever to pass the difficult final examination, the *agrégation*, and, consequently, the youngest philosophy teacher in France. She won second place in the highly competitive philosophy exam, losing by less than one-fiftieth of a percentage point to none other than Jean-Paul Sartre. The brilliant Sartre would soon become France's leading philosopher—and Simone's partner.

The story of Simone de Beauvoir cannot be told without considering her relationship with Sartre. In their lifetime together, they were icons of the Left Bank. And from the beginning, Sartre was smitten by this dark-haired beauty, with her high cheekbones, flashing blue eyes, and elegant, regal demeanor. "I was dead set on getting to know her because she was beautiful, because she had then, and still has the kind of face which attracts me," he told *Vogue* in 1965. "The miracle of Simone de Beauvoir is that she has the intelligence of a man and the sensitivity of a woman. In other words, she is everything I could want."

Simone was equally moved. For the first time she felt desired—and, more importantly, understood—a rare and powerful aphrodisiac. "Sartre always tried to see me as part of my own scheme of things, to understand me in the light of my own set of values and attitudes," she wrote.

However, Simone refused to marry Sartre, though he repeatedly asked. Deirdre Bair once asked her why, and Simone's response was simple: "Marriage was impossible. I had no dowry."

"Despite all the conventions she had flaunted so fearlessly [she was a true rarity at the time: a well-educated, independent woman], she was still cowed by the most important tenet of her social class," Bair observes. It did not matter that at the time of their conversation, Simone was an established feminist icon nearing the end of her life; she still saw some situations in her life through the lens of an adolescent. But there was another reason why she refused to marry: She never wanted to espouse the kind of dependence that marriage had created in her mother, her aunts, and the other women in her family.

In spite of this, their passion for one another was undeniable. As she recalled in her memoirs, in October 1929, as the pair sat on a stone bench in the Left Bank's majestic Luxembourg Gardens, Sartre turned, looked into Simone's eyes, and said, "Let's sign a two-year lease." And so they agreed to a two-year partnership, at the end of which they would each have the option to renew their commitment. They were together for the next fifty years.

Their unorthodox relationship—in addition to being unmarried, they allowed each other "contingent love affairs," as Sartre put it, with both men and women—was consistently questioned by the outside world. Simone, who, like the majority of first-wave feminists, was emancipated through entry into and acceptance in traditionally male professions, ultimately chose a career over children. Sartre continually defended their relationship in the press, saying, "What is unique between Simone de Beauvoir and me is the equality of our relationship."

Their commitment to one another was the stuff of legend, and their intellectual fireworks lit up the century. There was never enough time for the avalanche of ideas and words that these two committed to paper. While Sartre was a philosopher who felt at home with abstract concepts, Simone's source of creative impulse was guided by introspection. She sought solutions to her challenges through reading and writing. This intense self-examination led to many of her most compelling fictional characters—quite often women struggling to define themselves and their sense of personal responsibility in the face of preestablished social expectations. It also inspired the works that brought her the greatest fame: *L' Invitée* (*She Came to Stay*), *Le Sang des autres* (*The Blood of Others*), and *Quand prime le spirituel* (*When Things of*

The fact that we are human beings is infinitely more important than all the peculiarities that distinguish human beings from one another.

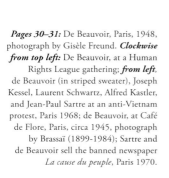

Pages 30–31: De Beauvoir, Paris, 1948, photograph by Gisèle Freund. *Clockwise from top left:* De Beauvoir, at a Human Rights League gathering; *from left,* de Beauvoir (in striped sweater), Joseph Kessel, Laurent Schwartz, Alfred Kastler, and Jean-Paul Sartre at an anti-Vietnam protest, Paris 1968; de Beauvoir, at Café de Flore, Paris, circa 1945, photograph by Brassaï (1899-1984); Sartre and de Beauvoir sell the banned newspaper *La cause du peuple*, Paris 1970.

the Spirit Come First) were publishing sensations. She won France's highest literary prize, the Prix Concourt, for 1954's *Les Mandarins* (*The Mandarins*).

The prism of existential philosophy shaped her ideas; she claimed that true freedom comes only when the individual recognizes and accepts it for others as well as for the self. "All I have to do to possess this fragment of the universe is truly cultivate it [like a garden]… No dimension can be assigned to the garden… It is not designed beforehand; it is I who chooses its site and limits," Simone wrote in the introduction to her book *Pyrrhus et Cinéas*. This concept stood in direct contrast to the social norms of the time. Much of the postwar world was not yet ready to accept a woman as an intellectual, even an unusually well educated one.

> To show your true ability is always, in a sense, to surpass
> the limits of your ability, to go a little beyond them:
> To dare, to seek, to invent; it is at such a moment that new
> talents are revealed, discovered, and realized.

Despite this forbidding social setting, Simone's literary reputation continued to grow. As she wrote more, she moved beyond her internal world to focus on the external and began to examine her place in society. As Bair relates, in reflecting on her position, Simone once told an interviewer it struck her by surprise "that the first thing I had to say was 'I am a woman.'"

So she set out to ascertain the condition of women in general, and the result was 1949's *Le Deuxième Sexe* (*The Second Sex*), one of the most important and far-reaching books on women ever published. Its thesis is basic: Because women are always considered in relation to men, every woman is inherently perceived as an outsider, what Simone termed "the Other." This, she asserted, is fundamental to the concept of oppression (and applicable to any oppressed identity, whether according to race, religion, or class). With great intellectual courage, Simone explored the lost or missing narrative of women through biology, history, and mythology. Her book attacked society's overarching patriarchal thinking but also asserted that women are so conditioned by culture that they consent to this subservience. One is not born a woman, she declared; one must become a woman.

The Second Sex's global impact is particularly extraordinary when one considers that Simone created this work of masterful scholarship in a vacuum, as a woman of a particular social and intellectual background with little firsthand knowledge of feminist movements within or outside her country. Within a decade of its publication, feminist action had become the most important outlet for Simone's energies and remained the dominating force in the last years of her life. Women around the world revered her, and her physical presence and written support guaranteed a forum for and elevated the visibility of any cause she embraced.

Notably, she allied herself with those fighting for the right to legal abortions in France at a time when contraception of any kind was illegal. Simone's influence led to the establishment of the first ministry of women's rights and the Commission Femme et Culture (Commission on Women and Culture), which members referred to as the "Commission Beauvoir" in honor of Simone. She generously donated time and money to fund shelters for battered and abused women. She also spoke out against governments with repressive policies and on behalf of people unjustly persecuted—including Algerians, Basque nationalists, homosexuals, Polish intellectuals, and Jews.

At the same time that she was a courageous and outspoken advocate for so many others, however, there were elements of her personal life that, somewhat surprisingly, reflect more of the patriarchal era in which she was raised than one might expect. It is worth noting, for example, that Simone often put herself and her work second to Sartre and his. Simone's pivotal role in Sartre's personal and professional life came into full view when their private letters were published posthumously. Through the letters, we have learned that without her, Sartre would have had no sounding board for his ideas, no critic for his writings, no coeditor for the magazine the couple cofounded with other intellectuals in 1945, *Les Temps modernes*, and no one to manage his relations with France's political and intellectual factions. Perhaps the best way to reconcile these personal struggles is to see them within the context of their historical time period; for under no circumstances should they overshadow her immeasurable contributions to the cultural landscape of our society.

For a writer to become an icon, she often must embody the spirit of the age. Simone is the quintessential personification of 1970s feminism. No other woman in contemporary literature has been so closely associated with the major events of her society. Simultaneously, she was, inarguably, very driven by her own internal voice. And her determination to live a life of passion—as articulated in her diary as a young woman—stayed with her throughout her life.

Upon her death, in 1986, newspaper headlines echoed the words that the French writer and feminist Elisabeth Badinter spoke at her funeral: "Women, you owe everything to her." She passed away on April 14, just eight hours before the anniversary of Sartre's death six years earlier. She was buried beside him. Feminists, scholars, former government ministers, the old and the young—along with a large delegation of African women in native dress—scattered single flowers and laid wreaths on her grave, in homage to the power of Simone's voice and ideas.

Through her tenacity, the little girl with "a man's brain" but "no dowry" turned adversity into good fortune, dedicating herself to her own education, self-determination, and shedding light on inequalities, wherever they lay. Even as she struggled, at times, to emancipate herself, she served as an inspiration to people around the world, and her ideas forever changed entrenched concepts of womanhood.

Wangari MAATHAI

(1940–2011)

Proud Daughter of Kenya

I visited Kenya for the first time in the summer of 2007. And what I encountered there—the culture, its breathtaking landscapes, its wondrous wildlife—forever altered the way I see the world. I tracked the nearly extinct cheetah, marveled at the thousands of wildebeests making their annual migration across the Mara River, and interviewed local rangers eager to preserve and promote their way of life. I left Kenya feeling that I had learned a great deal about this fascinating land.

Upon my return home, however, as I continued to read more about this beautiful country, I soon realized I'd missed a critical aspect of Kenyan history and culture. I had not been properly introduced to the remarkable story of Wangari Maathai, the Kenyan environmental and human rights activist—and the first African woman to win a Nobel Peace Prize. I promptly went about the business of educating myself and discovered one of the world's most inspirational women.

Wangari Maathai had a statuesque build, with broad shoulders and an even broader smile. She spoke with conviction in a deep and measured voice, and exuded a sense of personal power. She was a woman to be reckoned with: Despite imprisonment, charges of treason, and public ridicule, she never wavered in her mission to restore and protect Kenya's natural resources and to fight for human rights. When she shone too brightly or opposed the former Kenyan president Daniel arap Moi's draconian policies, she was lambasted as a "wayward" woman. As she noted in her aptly titled 2006 memoir, *Unbowed*, however, "When pressure is applied to me unfairly, I tend to dig in my heels and stand my ground—precisely the opposite of what those applying the pressure hope or expect."

Wangari founded the Green Belt Movement, a grassroots program that uses tree planting as an entry point to inspire larger discussions of self-determination, equity, and environmental conservation. The program began in Kenya and later spread to other African nations. Her dream

was to see her native land green and thriving once again. Over the years, thousands of women who believe in Wangari's vision have worked together to plant over thirty million trees.

Wangari's mission proved to be more controversial that one might think. While she set out to lead a movement to heal the wounds of the earth, the people of Kenya embarked on the difficult path of healing their own oppressive history of colonization. In planting trees, Wangari had also nurtured the seeds of democracy and personal empowerment.

Wangari was born in 1940 in a traditional mud-walled house in Nyeri in what was then British Kenya. The land was abundant with plants, the soil was rich, and drinking water was clean and plentiful. As was the custom, upon her birth, her Kikuyu community welcomed her with a special ritual: Her mother was fed bananas, sweet potatoes, lamb, and the juice of blue-purple sugarcane—all foods from the local land. Through her first drop of mother's milk, Wangari was also introduced to these tastes, thereby connecting her to the land and nature's magic.

Every experience has a lesson. Every situation has a silver lining.

However, her community's relationship to its land and customs was changing. For all the progress that British colonization was supposed to bring to Kenya, it often lowered the standard of living for its indigenous people. European settlers received title deeds, and some Kenyan tribes were relegated to living on designated reserves. British colonization had brought clear-cutting, logging, and hunting, which destroyed the natural ecosystem that helped gather and retain rainwater. Streams soon dried up, causing a shortage of drinking water. Fewer crops were cultivated, making less food available. The world that Wangari knew as a child was vanishing.

During the 1950s, Kenyan nationalists—known as Mau Mau—launched a war against the British for independence and land reclamation. The British reaction was harsh: Nearly one million Africans were sent to detention camps, where 100,000 of them perished. Wangari's own mother was forced into one of the government's emergency villages for seven long years.

By the time Wangari graduated from high school, in 1959, however, the colonial era was coming to an end, and a whole new world was opening up. Black Kenyans were allowed to vote in elections for the first time. And because Wangari was a good student, she was offered a scholarship by the Joseph P. Kennedy Jr. Foundation to study in the United States. At twenty, Wangari boarded a plane for the first time and headed to Atchison, Kansas, where she studied biological sciences at Mount St. Scholastica College (now Benedictine College). She went on to earn a master of science degree at the University of Pittsburgh in 1966.

Wangari returned to newly independent Kenya inspired by America's flourishing women's movement. As she noted in *Unbowed*, "I had higher aspirations and did not want to be compared with men of lesser ability and capacity. I wanted to be me." She earned a Ph.D. from the University of Nairobi in 1971, making her the first woman in East and Central Africa to earn a doctorate degree. She eventually became a senior lecturer and chair of the veterinary anatomy department at the University of Nairobi. (She was the first woman in Kenya to hold both posts.) Soon after, she married Mwangi Mathai who had also studied in America, and together they had three children. She shocked many around her by continuing to work throughout.

In 1976, Wangari became a member of the National Council of Women of Kenya, an organization formed in 1964 that was dedicated to women's political, economic, and social empowerment. Through the council, she saw firsthand the dire predicament of both her country's land and rural women. Trapped in poverty, these women had no clean drinking water, no crops for food, and no firewood. Wangari knew that the environment was directly related to their poor quality of life. As she said in the 2008 documentary *Taking Root: The Vision of Wangari Maathai*, "What we complain about are symptoms, and we need to understand the causes."

Wangari wrote in her memoir: "When what you remember disappears, you miss it and search for it." She dreamed of seeing her native land restored and believed change could come directly from the community. In 1977, she founded the Green Belt Movement, which proposed that women plant native seedlings to help restore the environment. For each tree planted, they were given four cents. Local communities, farms, schools, and churches took ownership of the movement, and soon tree nurseries sprang up all across Kenya. The Green Belt Movement established more than six hundred community-based networks.

But success ushered in new challenges for Wangari. She came home one day in July 1977 to find that her husband had left her. In her heart, she knew she had loved and supported him. But now she faced personal tragedy and financial insecurity. Heartbroken in her empty house, she searched for a broom. As she recalled in her memoir: "Sweep!" an inner voice ordered her. She spent the night sweeping up what her husband had left behind. As she swept the last bit of dust, she realized, "Picking myself up by my strings was a way of making sure that no matter how desperate a situation seemed, I didn't completely give up." This ability to extract positive lessons from life's challenges stayed with her throughout her life.

The courts and the press had a field day covering her divorce proceedings. As a successful woman, she threatened established notions of women's roles in Kenyan society. She was labeled too ambitious and educated to have sustained a good marriage. She was even threatened with contempt of court (after calling her judge corrupt) and sent to jail for a time as an example to other women. But she resolved "to hold my head high, put my shoulders back, and suffer with dignity: I would give every woman and girl reasons to be proud and never regret being educated, successful, and talented."

Meanwhile, the Green Belt Movement grew. In 1986, its leaders launched the Pan African Green Belt Network to share its unique tree planting–based initiative with leaders of other African countries. As a result, this approach was successfully implemented in Tanzania, Uganda, Malawi, Lesotho, Ethiopia, Zimbabwe, and elsewhere. In Kenya, it progressed from a tree-planting program into one that also educated and fostered ideas about personal responsibility, human rights, and gender relations. The movement also provided a forum for people to openly discuss the adverse effects of colonization and deforestation, many for the first time in their lives.

As the Green Belt Movement grew, so too did Wangari's influence and fame. A civic group in Kenya named her Woman of the Year in 1983. Then, in 1989, Diana, Princess of Wales, presented her with WomenAid International's prestigious Woman of the World Award. Other accolades came her way, including the coveted Goldman Environmental Prize, in 1991.

> For the stream to grow into a river, it must meet other tributaries and join them as it heads for a lake or the sea.

At the same time, pressure to keep her in check persisted. Kenya's President Moi, in office from 1978 to 2002, kept an iron grip on his country's power structure and sought to limit her role in the National Council of Women in Kenya by installing his own candidate. When that failed, Moi separated the council from the Green Belt Movement to reduce its donor support.

In the fall of 1989, the government announced plans to build a $200 million skyscraper in Uhuru Park, adjacent to Nairobi's central business district. Knowing that this massive structure would forever change the character of the park, Wangari wrote letters to politicians, nonprofit organizations, and newspapers opposing the development. President Moi retaliated by calling her group of activists a bunch of nagging divorcées, hoping to make an example of her.

Wangari received death threats. The Green Belt Movement was blacklisted. To Wangari, though, the struggle for Uhuru Park was a symbol of potential democracy, of ordinary citizens' ability to reclaim power by speaking out. After much international press coverage, foreign investors and donor governments backed out of the project. The standoff energized Kenya's people.

Under President Moi, Kenya had essentially become a one-party state. Opponents were often detained or imprisoned. Wangari and the Green Belt Movement joined others in pro-democracy activities and openly opposing Moi. To punish her, the police were ordered to arrest her. She was imprisoned on charges of spreading malicious rumors, sedition, and treason—the fifty-two-year-old arthritic Wangari was forced to spend sleepless nights in a cold, wet cell.

By the time of her hearing, Wangari had to be carried out of the courtroom to an ambulance. Outside the courtroom, she found an outpouring of support. Mothers in Action, a women's rights

Page 39: Maathai poses with the Nobel Diploma and Medal during a ceremony in Oslo's City Hall, 2004. *From left:* Then U.S. Senator Barack Obama and Maathai plant an African Olive Tree at Uhuru Park, 2006; Maathai and members of the Green Belt Movement, 2004; Maathai at Kagioini's Pentecostal Church.

group, raised a banner for her to see: "Wangari, Brave Daughter of Kenya, You Will Never Walk Alone Again." In Washington, D.C., members of the U.S. Senate Foreign Relations Committee applied pressure to Moi's regime, and charges against Wangari were eventually dropped.

In no time, Wangari was back in action, appealing to the government for the release of democratic activists. In 1992, she joined with mothers of political prisoners in Uhuru Park (later named Freedom Square) to stage a hunger strike. By the third day, their gathering had swelled to several hundred people. Many spoke out about their horrific experiences under the Moi regime.

On the fifth day of their protest, the police moved in. Batons were hurled at the protesters and gunshots filled the air. Wangari was knocked unconscious and taken to a hospital. But these mothers—including Wangari's own—had staged a powerful act of African defiance.

In the days that followed, the mothers sought refuge in a cathedral. When Wangari was released from the hospital, she returned to the protest. Eventually, the nonviolent protest paid off. In 1993, all but one of the fifty-two "political prisoner sons" were released.

Energized by the success, Wangari next helped create the movement for free and fair elections and coordinated seminars to teach Kenyans about the upcoming elections. In 2002, Moi was defeated in an election, and Wangari was elected to the Kenyan National Assembly with 98 percent of the vote. Thousands gathered in Uhuru Park to celebrate.

On October 8, 2004, Wangari learned she had been awarded the Nobel Peace Prize for her contribution to sustainable development, democracy, and peace. She was the first African woman and the first environmentalist to win the prize. Upon hearing the news, she celebrated the best way she knew how—by planting a seedling overlooking majestic Mount Kenya.

Wangari died of cancer in the fall of 2011 at the age of seventy-one. Her legacy, like the millions of trees she and others planted, lives on as a symbol of hope and determination to us all.

En Francia   — En México

Torera Conchita
CINTRÓN

(1922–2009)

The Lady Bullfighter, "The Blonde Goddess"

It was an August day and the sun was blazing. I stood on the arena's pounded dirt. There, in the mountain town of Ronda, Spain, home of the modern bullfight, I closed my eyes and traveled back in time, imagining a *corrida*, or bullfight, with the legendary Conchita Cintrón, the world's first celebrity *matadora*, or female bullfighter.

She fought in this ring years ago. As I stand here, I'm convinced I can feel the electrifying energy of her decades-old performance even now. In the distance, a band strikes up a paso doble. Ticket vendors hawk seats outside, and the crowd, filled with nervous excitement, makes its way inside. Pablo Picasso, Ernest Hemingway, and Orson Welles saunter over to their boxes, as do local politicians and judges. Inside the corral, the restless bulls start to pace—side to side, back and forth, over and over.

One testy bull rams the gate with his razor sharp horns, shining like black onyx daggers in the sun. In their private quarters, the *toreros*, or bullfighters, help one another drape the heavily embroidered parade cape over one shoulder and tuck it under the left arm. They cross themselves and wish each other good luck.

The clarion sounds, and the celebrated toreros strut into the plaza to a wild storm of applause, flowers, and streamers. There she is! Conchita Cintrón! Then the real drama begins: A magnificent, fifteen-hundred-pound bull charges in and attacks her flashing pink and yellow cape. The bull digs its hooves into the sand for a turn; with each cape pass, the skillful torera lets the animal come closer and closer. She takes your breath away.

Conchita—better known as La Diosa Rubia or The Blonde Goddess—was a child prodigy who broke into the male-dominated sport of bullfighting at age thirteen. She is said to have killed more than 750 bulls in her storied career at hundreds of events in Mexico, Peru, Venezuela, Colombia, Ecuador, Portugal, Spain, and France. As Orson Welles, one of Conchita's great admirers, wrote in the introduction to her 1968 autobiography, *Memoirs of a Bullfighter*: "Her record stands as a rebuke to every man of us who has ever maintained that a woman must lose something of her femininity if she seeks to compete with men. Conchita competed. Nobody was ever more perfectly feminine, and she triumphed absolutely in the most flamboyantly masculine of all professions."

Hers is a story of bravery and bashed stereotypes. Born in Antofagasta, Chile, in 1922, to a Puerto Rican father and an American mother, Conchita's parents called her Consuelo, which means "solace" in Spanish. She was born exactly one year after her parent's firstborn, Conchita's older brother, passed away. By the time she was three, her family had moved to Lima, Peru. Conchita loved Peru, which, as she put it in her memoir, "held on to traditions in spite of its modernity." The culture's social liberalism made it acceptable for a young girl to gravitate toward the country's prized traditional sport of bullfighting. By three, she had already ridden her first pony. At eleven, she came under the tutelage of Ruy da Cámara, a renowned former bullfighter of noble Portuguese lineage.

Conchita was trained in and mastered the two classic bullfighting styles—the traditional Spanish technique, on foot, and the Portuguese, called *rejoneador*, wherein a mounted bullfighter fights the bull on horseback. Both are beautiful dances between torero and bull. However, women have traditionally been prohibited from the former, as killing bulls on foot has been deemed too dangerous for their "delicate" natures. The bold and talented Conchita defied this tradition to resounding success in Latin America, but found resistance in the more conservative Spain.

> When the fighting bull is brave, he is an easy enemy to handle; so is a brave man. It is the coward man or bull who makes the unexpected move.

Conchita's parents supported their pioneering daughter's passion. As Conchita wrote in her autobiography, "My parents had an unwavering faith in all that I tried to do." When asked if it frightened her to see her daughter fight bulls, Conchita's mother replied, "Why would I be frightened when I am sure nothing will happen to her?"

Conchita inherited her athletic abilities from her father, who also supported her pursuits, but with markedly more hesitation. When it became clear Conchita wished to be a professional torera, her father tried to put his foot down and refused to let her train. But a one-day hunger strike persuaded him to reconsider. As Conchita's memoir notes: "I never wanted you, my only daughter, to be a torera," he told her, "but I felt that you will be one anyway. So I prefer that you have my blessing."

In addition to her family's support, Conchita was gifted with raw talent, impeccable timing, and an instinctively theatrical personality. She was also disciplined and well educated in her sport. Cámara always told her that if she wanted to be taken seriously, she had to fight serious bulls. At the same time, he warned that self-doubt was the torera's downfall. Like horses and dogs, he said, bulls can sense fear. And when a bullfighter knows that her opponent has recognized her fear, the anxiety only gets worse. Facing this fear head-on, Conchita spent months training on a friend's ranch. Soon enough, by age thirteen, she was ready for her first show at the historic Plaza de Acho in Lima.

Conchita was billed to participate first in the horse show and later as a *rejoneadora*. However, her horse missed a jump early on, throwing Conchita to the ground. Tears rolled down her face; the officials did not want to let her finish the show. If she was injured during the jumps, they said, she could not perform with the bulls. Ignoring their warnings, her mother and others consoled her and helped her into her *traje de corto* (riding costume). According to her memoir, her father told her, "Remember that whatever happens… I'll never fail you." Conchita performed splendidly with the bull, garnering resounding applause. From that day forward, she "delighted in thinking of the plazas that awaited me, of the horses I would train."

She soon embarked on a Latin American tour, joining the ranks of famed bullfighters. And while she was driven by her love of the sport, her day-to-day was more often than not decidedly unglamorous: nights at dingy inns infested with bedbugs and frogs, mornings at boardinghouses without running water, and cars that broke down at the worst of times. But she loved it nevertheless. "I was finally experiencing what had formerly been anecdotes in the lives of others," she wrote in her memoir.

Her first bullfight was in Guadalajara, Mexico, in 1937, on the Saint's Day of the Conchitas. She made the paseo to the tune of "Las Mañanitas," the traditional Mexican birthday song, and handled the bull with elegance and ease. At the end, doves were released from the stands and hats and bonbons were tossed at her horse's feet. *El Redondel* declared: "She is more a 'phenomenon' in the truest senses of the word… Don't you think it extraordinary that this little girl of fifteen, who looks as if she were made of porcelain, not only bullfights like an angel, but is an expert horsewoman and first-class rejoneadora? Make way for Conchita!"

Offers soon poured in, guaranteeing engagements in major Latin American cities, including Quito, Ecuador; Caracas, Venezuela; and Bogota, Colombia. She became the darling of the circuit. Fans fell in love. Newspapers claimed she was the greatest bullfighting spectacle ever seen. At one particularly memorable event in Bogota, she performed in a charity show for thirty thousand children, free of charge. At another, fifteen thousand spectators filled a plaza. Thousands more who could not get tickets stormed the police guarding the entrances.

Appearing in Lisbon, Portugal, and Spain proved to be more of a challenge. While she met several notables—including the Count and Countess of Barcelona, the Duke of Alba, and the Duchess of Santoña—Portuguese horsemen refused to appear with her, which automatically eliminated her from the rings. Cámara was dispatched to plead her case to the authorities. The ministers asked that an invitation be sent to all rejoneadors; if they all refused to appear with her, she would be granted permission to perform alone. Not a single person replied. Finally, one of Cámara's friends, an old retired rejoneador, offered to accompany Conchita in the paseo. Once again, she dazzled her audience.

Her great dream, however, was to conquer Spain. Eventually, she was invited to fight at the Seville Fair—but only if she performed on horseback, rather than on foot, in keeping with Spanish law. When the trumpets sounded for the kill, the heartbroken Conchita could not go through with it; instead, she dismounted from her trembling white stallion and left the ring.

> 66 Toreros seem to remain youthful more than anyone else; the men of the arena live on hopes and illusions, and those who live that way do not age. 99

Pages 44–45: Cintrón prepares to kill a bull from horseback, Mexico City, 1942. **Clockwise from top left:** The Blonde Goddess, circa 1957; Cintrón, poised for the fatal thrust between the bull's shoulder blades, Mexico City, 1942; a formal portrait of Cintrón.

Cámara, the Peruvian ambassador, and the minister of foreign affairs worked tirelessly to get permission for Conchita to fight on foot. Finally she was allowed to, but only at private corridas sponsored by a government-run charity organization. While she received no fee for fighting on foot, her memoir reveals she felt "it was a thousand times more fun to fight on foot for nothing than to perform only on horseback, however well paid."

She continued with charity performances in San Sebastián, Madrid, and Oropesa. But just as new doors had begun opening for her, another promptly slammed in her face. Under growing pressure from the authorities, she was once again banned from dismounting in the arena. Disappointed, she left for Morocco to fight under the invitation of the Muslim head of state. She was assured that nothing would happen if she were to dismount from her horse. After all, His Royal Highness, the caliph, wished to see her on foot. Unfortunately, the Spanish protectorate authorities felt differently. Right after the bullfight, she was slapped with a steep fine. There was also a warning: If she ever got off her horse in the ring again, she would be expelled from all of Spain's arenas. Dejected, she left for France, where she performed at the fetes of Arles, Bordeaux, Marseille, and Béziers, among others.

Of course, one can only keep a lady waiting for so long. In October 1949, at the fair in Jaén, Spain, Conchita made a decision that led to one of the most dramatic events in bullfighting history. That day, the stands overflowed with fans. Conchita, on horseback and dressed in a magnificent traje de corto, stopped her stallion beneath the presidential box. She looked at the bull before her, then looked toward the president and touched the horse with her spurs. According to her memoir, the crowd, sensing what was about to happen, stood and shouted, "Señor Presidente, let her fight on foot!" But the president cut through the commotion with a firm and final no gesture.

Impassioned, Conchita dismounted and grabbed the sword from her stunned understudy, who was assigned to kill the bull. Then, as the bull charged, Conchita dramatically dropped the sword into the sand, stepped out of its path, and simulated the kill by touching the bull's shoulders with her fingers as it rushed by. The crowd exploded in cheers, hurling red carnations and hats at her feet.

She was arrested ringside. The crowd yelled, "*Perdon! Perdon!* If they take you to jail, we'll come after you." With fans on the verge of a full-scale riot, the regional governor pardoned her on the spot. That day, although she was awarded the highest honor of the ring—the bull's ears and tail—Conchita bid farewell to the spectators and the sport in tears. But she never regretted her last moments in the arena; she had accomplished what she set out to do.

In 1951, two years after her retirement at age twenty-seven, Conchita married a Portuguese nobleman, Francisco de Castelo Branco, who was Cámara's nephew and a successful businessman. She spent the rest of her life in Lisbon, where she raised five children and bred hardy Portuguese water dogs. In her retirement, she served as an unofficial diplomat, working with the Peruvian embassy in Portugal and as a correspondent for Mexican and Peruvian newspapers. She died on February 17, 2009.

On reflection, bullfighting may also serve as an apt analogy for life. As a torera, Conchita recognized and embraced life's emotions as they came. She shows us that we too can face fear head-on—dance with it, turn aside when it charges our way, and ultimately conquer it. Conchita was brave enough to fight for and grab hold of experiences that often unleashed a torrent of varying emotions and states of being—despair, excitement, failure, triumph, and faith—often all at once with the pass of her cape.

In bullfighting culture, it is customary to call out "*Mucho, mucho!*" when one sees something grand in the bullring. Conchita Cintrón offered her sport grace under fire, making an indelible mark on both bullfighting and the world's perception of women. To the Blonde Goddess, we say, "Mucho, mucho!"

66 The arena to me is a microcosm of the world. Within its small circle one finds life, death, ambition, despair, success, failure, faith... all condensed into a single afternoon or even a single moment. 99

Conchita Cintrón

Ella FITZGERALD

(1917–1996)

The Eternal Child of Jazz

I was reading a book at my desk one afternoon about the First Lady of Song, when a fact I spotted jolted me upright in my chair. Ella Fitzgerald, perhaps the most celebrated female recording artist in American history, had lived on Whittier Drive in Beverly Hills, just a few blocks away from me.

I immediately jotted down her exact address, grabbed my purse, and drove down the hill to the house she had once called home. I couldn't believe it. For years I have parked my car just a few yards away from her place to meet friends for hikes in our neighborhood. I've often pointed out how much I love the weeping willow in the front yard.

It isn't where you came from, it's where you're going that counts.

"Look, it's as if the leaves sway, shimmer, and dance with the breeze," I always say.

Sway, shimmer, and dance are appropriate verbs to use for this musical icon. Her love of music and her God-given, one-of-a-kind voice were the source of her own life's joy—and thrilled millions of fans around the globe. "To live is to perform; there is no other meaning or reason for being alive," is how Stuart Nicholson described Ella's relationship to her work in his 1994 book, *Ella Fitzgerald: A Biography of the First Lady of Jazz*. In a career spanning six decades, she sold more than forty million albums and earned almost every imaginable honor, including thirteen Grammy Awards, a Kennedy Center Award, the National Medal of Arts, as well as honorary doctorates in music from Yale, Dartmouth, and Princeton.

Fate smiled on Ella from the start of her career. Doors seemed to open easily for her; sometimes, as the story goes, to the envy of her contemporary female vocalists. As Nicholson recounts, one day early in Ella's career, the great jazz singer Billie Holiday walked into Harlem's Savoy Ballroom to measure up the plump newcomer singing with the celebrated Chick Webb's band. According to Charles Linton, Ella's fellow singer at the time, "A great band like that with Ella?" the sultry Holiday snapped in disbelief. "That bitch." She turned around and walked out.

Ella herself was no diva. If anything, she was known for her childlike qualities. According to Nicholson, Ella skipped rope backstage to keep in shape and was happy to let others organize her life—ordering meals, booking gigs, and so on. All she cared about was making music; everything else amounted to petty details.

Ella's youthful innocence was nowhere more evident than in her voice. Music critics and writers have claimed that her perpetually youthful timbre and the uncomplicated emotional tone of her voice allowed her songs to achieve a level of disarming honesty. "The values she communicated were simple, even optimistic; her yearning became the adolescent's yearning," notes Nicholson.

Ella's talent was shockingly raw. She never took a voice lesson or studied music. In fact, upon receiving her honorary doctorate of music from Yale, she summed up the accolade with humility: "Not bad for someone who only studied music to get that half credit in high school."

Born to an unwed mother, Temperance (known as Tempie), in 1917, baby Ella moved from Newport News, Virginia, to Yonkers, New York, with her mother. Children in her neighborhood remembered Ella shaking her shoulders and dancing—her hoop earrings dangling as she made her way to school. She and her friend Charles Gulliver used to sneak into the Savoy Ballroom to learn the latest dance steps. By the time she was fifteen, Ella was scoring dance gigs in neighborhood clubs. In fact, she never intended to become a professional singer. When seventeen-year-old Ella entered the famous Apollo Theater talent contest, she registered as a dancer.

But fate interceded on November 21, 1934. A couple of days before the contest, Ella discovered that she had stiff competition in the dance category. She abruptly resubmitted her paperwork to enter the contest as a singer, changing the trajectory of the rest of her life.

She was not the typical teenage vocalist. Two years earlier, Tempie had died suddenly of a heart attack. It is unclear what happened to Ella while under the care of her stepfather immediately after her mother's death, but the situation was tenuous enough for Tempie's sister in Harlem to take Ella into her own custody. Ella soon dropped out of school and started living on the streets, eating and sleeping whenever she could. Disheveled, unwashed, and overweight, she was hardly the image of a charming and glamorous entertainer who would dazzle the judge at the Apollo talent contest. That November evening, though, she brought the house down and was declared the winner. Ella Fitzgerald the singer was born.

About this time, Chick Webb, one of the most popular swing bandleaders in Harlem, was looking to add a female vocalist to his lineup. Ella's name was recommended. But when Webb asked for her phone number, he was told she didn't have one. When he searched for her address, that didn't exist either. Webb was told that Ella played on 125th Street every day, so he sent someone to find her there. At first, looking at the shabbily dressed Ella, Webb was not impressed. But once she opened her mouth and began to sing, he recognized the talent before him.

Webb was struck by the then eighteen-year-old Ella's ability to memorize lyrics during rehearsals in just a few hours. Then she would come back at night and sing the tunes perfectly. Her debut with his band was a huge success. On July 10, 1935, Ella began a weeklong singing engagement with the Chick Webb band. "It takes Ella Fitzgerald to send the audience into a vociferous display of enthusiasm," read the glowing review in *New York Age*. Six months later, her performance at the Savoy Ballroom turned even more heads: "Unheralded and practically unknown right now, but what a future… one of the best femme hot warblers…

and there's no reason why she shouldn't be just about the best in time to come," raved the American jazz writer George T. Simon in *Metronome* magazine.

Simon proved to be right. In less than four years, Ella rose from near obscurity to undeniable stardom. At the age of twenty-one, she was a singing sensation with a number of hits under her belt. By 1938, she was already being hailed as "the First Lady of Swing."

One secret to Ella's success was her near-perfect pitch. She intrinsically knew the precise relationship of every other note to the note sounded. And she had an improvisational style that made words swing. The singer-songwriter Mel Tormé, always a fan of Ella's, noted that she could compress or elongate particular words in a lyric so subtly that the words would gain a momentum of their own. Also, her knack for always singing perfectly in tune helped her become one of the great scat singers of the jazz era. As Tormé observed, Ella spouted out random notes in a matter of milliseconds with perfect intonation and rhythmic ease—a skill very few could replicate.

Those close to her assert that she always had a song in mind and constantly hummed melodies to herself. "Music comes out of her. When she walks down the street, she leaves notes," Jimmy Rowles, Ella's pianist and accompanist for thirty years, once said in an interview.

But all did not come easy to this songstress. She was a young girl in a man's world, and she had to prove herself night after night in front of demanding audiences. In the chauvinistic and notoriously precarious jazz world, Nicholson writes, "a woman has to prove herself more than an equal of her male contemporaries to become accepted in their domain."

Racial discrimination was also rampant during most of her long career. By the 1940s, Ella had broken through to white audiences, but she still had to find a seat in the blacks-only train car when she headed south for a concert. Once, after hours of standing in a train waiting for a seat to open in her designated area, she moved over to take a seat in the whites-only section. The conductor promptly tried to throw her out of the section and was stopped only by the objections of several sailors seated nearby. Another time, while headed to Australia for a concert series, Ella and her party were bumped from a connecting flight in Hawaii to make room for white patrons.

After Chick Webb passed away, in 1939, Ella began to tour the country on her own, taking over for him as bandleader. During this period, around 1941, Ella married Benjamin Kornegay, a local dockworker. Their union did not last long. Unbeknownst to her, Benjamin had a criminal record and planned on taking advantage of Ella's growing wealth. In 1947, she was unlucky in love again. Ella married the bass player Ray Brown. They adopted her half-sister's son and raised him as their own, but her constant touring and their unpredictable work schedules drove a wedge into the relationship.

> **I stole everything
> I ever heard,
> but mostly I stole
> from the horns.**

Pages 52–53: Fitzgerald, circa late 1960s.
Clockwise from top left: Fitzgerald leaving Nice
Côte d'Azur airport to go to a jazz festival
in Antibes Juan-les-Pins, 1964; a poster for
a 1968 concert; Fitzgerald and Louis Armstrong
at a recording session for Decca in New York,
1950; Marilyn Monroe and Fitzgerald
at Hollywood's Tiffany Club, 1954; Fitzgerald
performing, circa 1960; the singer in 1960.

One of Ella's most important career moves was her successful transition from swing to bebop—the fast-emerging, revolutionary movement in jazz. This is showcased on her hit 1945 record, "Flying Home," which critics hail as one of the finest jazz vocals of all time. The following year, her collaboration with the singer and trumpet player Louis Armstrong on two records and her tour with the trumpeter Dizzy Gillespie, who had become bebop's front man, sealed her position in this new jazz era.

Ella now sang to standing-room-only crowds in posh nightclubs and traveled in first class. By 1949, she was earning an astounding $3,000 a week. During this period, Ella became a notable interpreter of the Great American Songbook, which represented the best American songs of the twentieth century. Landmark albums such as 1950's *Ella Sings Gershwin* and 1956's *Ella Fitzgerald Sings the Cole Porter Songbook*, one of the best-selling jazz albums of all time, highlighted her artistic virtuosity.

A number of performances stand out in Ella's career: One was her gig as the first African American to sing at the swanky Mocambo club in Hollywood. The great Marilyn Monroe, a devoted fan, actually gave the club's owner an incentive to book Ella. She promised to sit front and center at her performances every night if Ella was given the chance to sing there. Marilyn told the owner the press would go wild—and they did. Ol' Blue Eyes was also a fan and made history with Ella when they performed a chemistry-charged duet on *The Frank Sinatra Show* in 1957. Sinatra even gave up his own dressing room to her for the TV show. And recordings of Ella's 1958 performance at the Teatro Sistina in Rome were discovered and released thirty years after the event—and soon topped the charts.

In her heyday, Ella's whirlwind schedule had her performing all over the world, often doing brutal one-nighters in one country followed by another show in another country the next night. Her younger backup musicians sometimes wondered aloud how she had the stamina to do it all. In 1986, Ella underwent quintuple coronary bypass surgery, but within a year she was performing once again. She continued to suffer health problems, however, as diabetes and circulatory problems slowed her down. She experienced impaired vision and she had a toe amputated. But even then she rebounded, accepting awards and continuing concerts.

A sense of humor helped her cope. As Nicholson notes, in her 1988 appearance at the Hollywood Bowl, Ella took a tumble but jokingly said, "It's okay. I'm okay. I'll just sing from down here." Some in the audience had left at intermission, thinking she was not in shape to return for the second half. But she bounced back onstage with the song "I Fell for You."

In 1989, the Society of Singers created a trophy to honor her for a lifetime of achievement, dubbing it the Ella. Bill Cosby hosted the occasion, and her friends Barbra Streisand, Quincy Jones, Clint Eastwood, and Jimmy Stewart toasted her. The following year, she presented the Ella to Frank Sinatra. That same year, she took part in Quincy Jones's *Back on the Block* album. Ella was unstoppable.

She loathed retirement. Performing was so much a part of her makeup that she continued a forty-weeks-a-year touring schedule under her doctor's supervision. Music and performance seemed to replace what was missing in her private life. She and her adopted son did not enjoy a close relationship, and her third marriage had also ended in divorce.

The only thing better than singing is more singing.

The First Lady of Jazz, often insecure personally, seemed to find her security and joy onstage. The mature singer who delivered such a memorable rendition of George Gershwin's "Someone to Watch Over Me" had been orphaned as a child, without anyone watching over her from a young age, and her anxieties about love and attachment resurfaced often. Curiously, even after decades of accolades and admiration, Ella also suffered from performance anxiety. As Nicholson relates, before going onstage, she would take a peek at the audience and say, "I hope they like me." But she felt truly loved onstage.

In 1953, music and jazz luminaries converged to celebrate Ella's first two decades in music. That evening she received eighteen awards and a plaque commemorating her sales of more than twenty-two million records for the Decca label. Her acceptance speech revealed her deepest needs: "I guess what everyone wants more than anything else is to be loved. And to know that you love me for my singing is too much for me. Forgive me if I don't have all the words. Maybe I can sing it and you'll understand."

Ella found in music the perfect vehicle to express her joy. During her half-century career, she recorded more than two hundred albums. As Nicholson notes, Ella at her best was "bringing pleasure to others by bringing pleasure to herself." Her joy in making music was so strong that she continued to perform well into the 1990s, even when she suffered from poor health. She said music was good medicine.

Ella's journey—from poverty and segregation to the stages of the world's most magnificent concert halls—is the embodiment of the American Dream. She died at age seventy-nine in Beverly Hills, California, but lives on through her music as each new generation discovers and is inspired by her genius.

Helen SUZMAN

(1917–2009)

Conscience of a Nation

Growing up in South Africa during the apartheid era, members of Helen Suzman's family sometimes received racist phone calls at home from cowardly cranks. These callers were angry at the family's antiapartheid politics and thought the anonymous, late-night calls would intimidate the Suzmans. They were wrong.

In fact, Helen Suzman, a wife, a mother, and a well known member of the South African Parliament, used a special trick. "She had a police whistle, and she would blow into the mouthpiece of the phone when she got those awful calls," her nephew Stephen Suzman told me years later. She was, without a doubt, a force to be reckoned with.

Madeleine Albright, the former U.S. secretary of state, has said, "The first step to success for women and girls is to learn how to interrupt in the classroom or workplace. A woman who is afraid to interrupt may never be heard, and only by being heard can we make a difference." Helen Suzman did just that. For thirteen years, from 1961 to 1974, she was the only member of South Africa's Parliament who openly challenged apartheid policy. This petite, indefatigable woman was regularly jeered at and taunted in Parliament. "You are the biggest political enemy of this country," she was once told. But Helen was undaunted.

During her thirty-six years in Parliament (1953–89), she was the voice for those who were unjustly imprisoned, those who didn't have the right to vote, and those who were denied freedom of movement and employment under the infamous "pass laws." She visited those displaced in slums and black townships and prisoners locked away out of sight.

Helen's regular visits to one particular prisoner are especially well documented. Nelson Mandela credits Helen with helping to improve his living conditions while in prison. "It was an odd and wonderful sight to see this courageous woman peering into our cells and strolling

around our courtyard," Mandela wrote in his autobiography, *Long Walk to Freedom*. "She was the first and only woman ever to grace our cells." His second wife, Winnie Madikizela-Mandela, also cited Helen's visits in an interview with the BBC in 1986: "Had it not been for her lone voice in Parliament those years, the rest of the world would never have known what was going on in this country."

"She was independent-minded, had a very sharp tongue and a very sharp wit," recalled Stephen Suzman, an accomplished landscape designer who now lives in San Francisco. These qualities—and her mastery of facts—were her real weapons. As related in her memoir, *In No Uncertain Terms*, once, in 1966, when the Afrikaner prime minister Hendrik Frensch Verwoerd told her that he had written her off, she promptly retorted, "And the whole world has written you off." Another time, a furious National Party cabinet minister admonished her in Parliament for her probing inquiries, shouting, "You put these questions just to embarrass South Africa overseas." She calmly replied, "It is not my questions that embarrass South Africa—it is your answers."

It is the answers, not the questions, that are embarrassing.

So how did she develop such a thick skin and quick tongue? Who was she before she rose up to defy all the political heavyweights and take a stand for dignity and equality for all citizens?

Helen Suzman was born Helen Gavronsky on November 7, 1917, in Germiston, a gold-mining town on the outskirts of Johannesburg. Her father emigrated from a Lithuanian shtetl to escape the pogroms and seek a better life in South Africa. Helen's mother, who had also emigrated from Eastern Europe, died soon after her birth, and her father remarried when she was nine years old. As Helen wrote in her memoir, "There was, obviously, an absence of maternal affection. Perhaps that engendered in me the strong spirit of independence which persists to this day." She inherited her father's stamina, but her parents did not encourage liberal ideas at home. Helen's father enrolled her (and her sister) in the Parktown Convent in Johannesburg to get a good education.

At nineteen, Helen dropped out of the University of Witwatersrand, where she was studying economics, and married Moses Meyer Suzman, known as Mosie, an eminent cardiologist, then thirty-three years old. As a young white South African housewife, she lived a privileged life. She gave birth to her first child, Frances, at twenty-one. Soon after, she went back to school to finish her undergraduate degree and, by 1943, had given birth to her second daughter, Patricia. Later, she became interested in politics while teaching economic history at

Witwatersrand University. She became a member of the executive council of the South African Institute of Race Relations, and her research into the many restrictions on and difficulties of urban blacks motivated her move into politics.

In late 1952 Helen was asked to run for Parliament. With her husband's encouragement, she ran and was elected to the House of Assembly as the member for Houghton, a prosperous and heavily Jewish suburb near Johannesburg. For the next three and a half decades, she spent nearly six months of each year in Cape Town (a thousand miles from Johannesburg) as a parliamentary member.

Her main focus in Parliament was race discrimination, the rule of law, and the administration of justice. She was part of the liberal wing of the United Party, which opposed many of the National Party's bills that, in tandem, made up key elements of the socially engineered apartheid system, such as Prime Minister Verwoerd's Bantu Education Bill, which intentionally condemned black children to inferior education—thereby relegating them to inferior jobs as well. Her United Party also opposed the first forced removal of some sixty thousand black South Africans from urban areas near white suburbs of Johannesburg to a place fifteen miles away that is now part of Soweto. Their houses were razed to the ground and they themselves transported to new townships that lacked even the most basic infrastructure.

Helen's first major act of defiance came in 1953 when the United Party supported the Separate Amenities Bill. This measure asked for separate but unequal amenities for blacks, Indians, and whites. She refused to vote for the bill, but it was passed into law.

As she recalled in her memoir, in 1957 during parliamentary debate on the State-Aided Institutions Bill, which permitted museum, gallery, and library authorities to set separate hours for various racial groups, Helen had a heated row with Sannie van Niekerk, a woman who represented one of the few rural seats held by the United Party. During a caucus, the petulant van Niekerk said, "Well, I don't know about Mrs. Suzman, but when I go to a museum, I don't like it if some strange black man rubs himself up against me." Suzman didn't miss a beat, replying, "Don't you mind if some strange white man rubs himself up against you?" A roar of laughter ensued.

Several other discriminatory bills followed that Helen again vehemently opposed. She denounced the government's plan to induce blacks into forced labor with subhuman working conditions, as well as the restrictions on blacks who wanted to study in white universities. Perhaps the most outrageous scheme of all was the plan to take South African citizenship away from blacks ethnically connected with Bantustans, independent black rural homelands to be established through a forced resettlement program, leaving a white majority in South Africa. Some blacks in the urban areas would be considered "temporary sojourners" and would have tribal representatives only. Helen visited the resettlement areas and reported on the horrific conditions to both the press and Parliament—people were living in tents or shacks without piped water, health clinics, shops, or schools.

I stand for simple justice, equal opportunity, and human rights—the indispensable elements in a democratic society—and well worth fighting for.

Helen's opposition to these racist laws created tension within her own United Party. In 1959 she and eleven colleagues resigned from it and formed the Progressive Party, which advocated total opposition to apartheid. By 1960 mass protest meetings organized by blacks had led the government to declare a state of emergency. Sixteen hundred people were imprisoned without trial. The United Nations Security Council condemned the South African response, and boycotts by the rest of the world began. It was also during this period that Helen began visiting detainees. As related in her memoir, when she drove out to the Central Prison in Pretoria with her friend Kathleen Mitchell, she warned: "Katie, if I don't come out within an hour, start screaming."

Tensions escalated further, and soon the so-called ninety-day detention law was passed, in which the minister of justice and police and senior police officials were given power to imprison anyone, at any time, for ninety days without a trial; no emergency state declaration was necessary. Often prisoners were tortured into giving confessions, and their whereabouts were kept secret, even from their families. Again, Helen had sharp exchanges with her fellow Parliament members. But with the growing opposition, even more severe laws were passed to crush any resistance. In the 1961 elections, Helen was the only member of Parliament able to keep her seat under the Progressive Party platform—and so began her thirteen lonely years as the sole voice of dissent.

With no speechwriter on her staff, Helen spent hours working on speeches addressing Parliament, protest meetings, university gatherings, and party public meetings. Some newspapers sprang to her defense. *The New York Times* commented in 1966 that Helen "represents more South Africans than all the other members of Parliament combined." That same year, the headline of a black South African newspaper, *The World*, dubbed her "Our Hero" upon her reelection to Parliament, noting that there was much jubilation in Soweto and other black townships.

At the beginning of the 1963 parliamentary session, she quoted a defiant antiapartheid speech made by Nelson Mandela at a 1962 trial—he was accused of inciting a strike and leaving South Africa illegally—that resulted in a five-year sentence. As related in her memoir, a National Party member, who spoke after her, remarked sarcastically, "I want to congratulate the Honorable Member for Houghton, Mrs. Suzman, on her new leader, Mandela." Knowing that Mandela's

> " I represent all the enlightened people in this country, and that's a fine thing to be able to do. It infuriates my opponents when I say this, but it is true. "

words faced strict censorship, Helen chose to subvert restrictions on free speech by repeating his words here, knowing that anything recorded in Parliament could be published by the press.

Helen made her first visit to Mandela at the Robben Island prison—which is surrounded by strong currents, freezing water, and sharks—about five and a half miles from the mainland of Cape Town, in 1967. There were rumors about the harsh treatment of prisoners by wardens, and Helen wanted to see the conditions for herself. There, in a single cell, through iron bars she caught sight of Mandela. They shook hands through the bars, and he lost no time in detailing all the hardships endured by the prisoners. After their first meeting, Helen wrote a formal letter to the minister of justice; conditions soon improved. Mandela, in turn, sent word to thank her. She reported her conversation with Mandela to the press, and as related in her memoir, "said I was convinced that his presence at the negotiating table was essential for a peaceful future."

Those who can talk must continue to talk.

This was the beginning of a decades-long friendship between the two. Although Mandela was in prison for some twenty-seven years, Helen noted in her memoir that his spirit was unbroken and that "there was nothing deferential in his relationship with prison authorities." On a visit to him in July 1989, six months before his release, the world's most famous political prisoner asked Helen to autograph a book she had brought him. He, in return, autographed *Fear No Evil*, a book by Natan Sharansky, the famous Russian dissident and human rights activist, who was in prison and the gulags from 1977 to 1986. In her memoir, Helen described the autographed book as one of her most prized possessions.

"Shortly after being released from prison, Mandela called Helen to ask her why she hadn't come to visit him yet," her nephew Stephen fondly recalled. The friendship between the two political heavyweights continued until the very end. After Mandela became the first black president of South Africa, in 1994, he sent a helicopter for Helen so that she could join him for the signing of the new constitution, and he was present with the rest of her family members on Helen's ninety-first birthday.

As Helen noted in her memoir, her opposition to sanctions clouded her relationships with many people overseas and many blacks in South Africa. She wrote articles for *The New York Times Magazine*, *The Washington Post*, and *The Times of London* in opposition to economic sanctions against South Africa. She believed these punitive measures would cause her country's economy to shrink, only increasing poverty and unemployment, especially for the black population. Mandela and Desmond Tutu (who Helen says in her memoir referred to her as his "dear child") both disagreed on this point with her.

By 1989, she was nearing seventy-two years of age and ready to retire. Before leaving Parliament, Helen visited with F. W. de Klerk, the country's president at the time. In a conversation related in her memoir, "Don't forget," she told him, "that checks and balances are necessary to prevent abuse of power by the majority."

"Ah. I see you have become a Nat," de Klerk responded.

"Not at all," she replied with her characteristic wit, "you have become a Young Prog."

After leaving Parliament, Helen continued her contributions to the civic life of South Africa. She served as president of the South African Institute of Race Relations from 1991 to 1993, was part of the independent electoral commission overseeing the country's first democratic election, in 1994, and was a member of the Human Rights Commission from 1995 to 1998. The Helen Suzman Foundation was established in 1993 to further the values espoused by Helen throughout her public life and in her devotion to public service.

Over the years, the international community recognized Helen's commitment to justice with multiple awards and honors. She won the United Nations Human Rights Award in 1978. She was designated by Queen Elizabeth II as Honorary Dame Commander of the Civil Division of the Order of the British Empire in 1989. Her unyielding courage in the fight for racial equality earned her two nominations for the Nobel Peace Prize. And leading universities, including Oxford, Cambridge, Columbia, Harvard, Brandeis, Witwatersrand, Yale, and Cape Town, conferred some twenty-seven honorary doctorates on her.

One 1966 incident related in Helen's memoir seems to capture her impact. At the height of the student demonstrations in Cape Town, Robert F. Kennedy, then a U.S. senator, gave a rousing speech:

> "Few will have the greatness to bend history itself,
> but each of us can work to change a small portion of events…
> Each time a man stands up for an ideal or acts to improve
> the lot of others, or strikes out against injustice, he sends forth
> a tiny ripple of hope… those ripples build a current which
> can sweep down the mightiest walls of oppression."

On his return to America, Kennedy wrote a letter to Helen praising her efforts and, most importantly, her persistence. Surely Helen, who was often called "the conscience of her nation," was that ripple of hope for millions. This brave icon was a key leader in the struggle that brought down the walls of South African oppression. Helen Suzman died on New Year's Day in 2009, at the age of ninety-one.

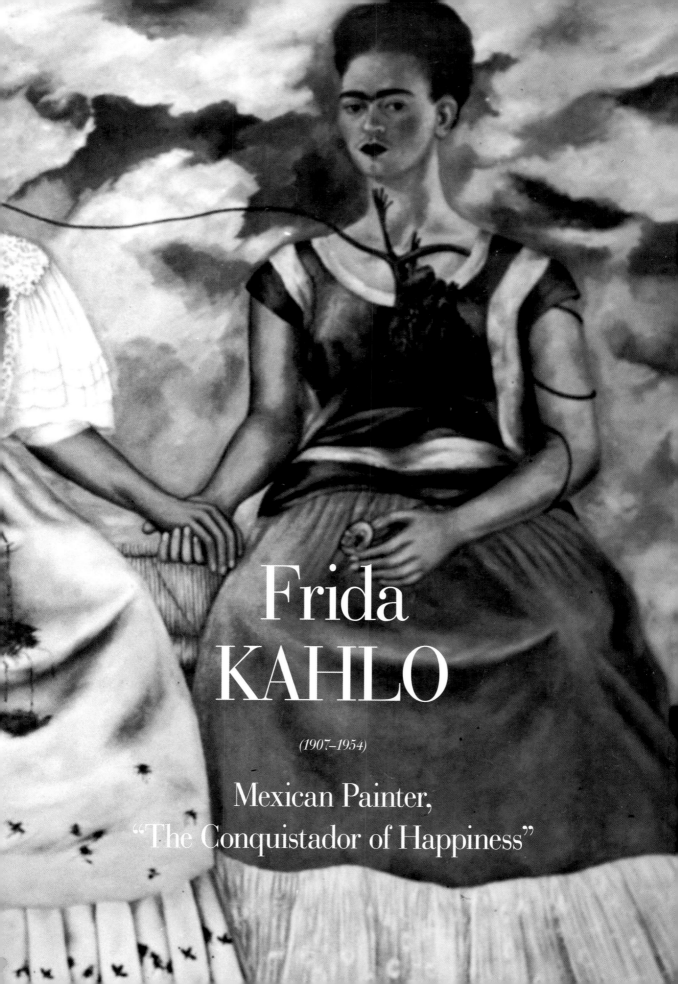

Frida
KAHLO

(1907–1954)

Mexican Painter,
"The Conquistador of Happiness"

The first time I saw her was in a souvenir shop in the historic city of San Miguel de Allende, Mexico. Her face was partially hidden by a beaded curtain hanging in the entrance. The next day, as I strolled along the jacaranda-lined side streets off the main square, I saw her again in an art gallery. She had a steely gaze and the hint of a mustache. Her eyebrows formed an unbroken line across her forehead, and above it stood a crown of braids with bright ribbons and a bougainvillea blossom clasped on one side. She wore native Mexican dress: an embroidered blouse and a ruffled long skirt. She was Frida Kahlo.

I quickly realized that her face permeated this town: It was printed on T-shirts and tote bags, embossed on stationery, even stenciled on a lamp shade. Yes, I had seen her image before. In the United States, her striking face stares out coolly from a thirty-four-cent stamp—making her the first Hispanic woman to receive such an honor. And I would soon discover that there are some sixty thousand Web sites dedicated to the subject of Frida Kahlo. But it wasn't until my visit to San Miguel de Allende that I realized how fully our global society has embraced her. We seem to be in the midst of Fridamania.

Few artists have captured the public's imagination like Frida Kahlo. Her paintings explore unflinchingly private themes: She charted her raw emotions throughout her lifetime, even recording the toll that some thirty-two medical operations and multiple miscarriages had taken on her body. No woman before her had depicted such themes visually.

Some knew her as the vivacious wife of the larger-than-life Mexican muralist Diego Rivera, who was twenty-one years her senior. But Rivera's world fame never overshadowed Frida. The light that attracted people to her came wholly from the force of her own personality. She had intense, intelligent eyes; a contagious, full-bellied laugh; and a sensuously low and raspy voice. Although she had a regal carriage, she cursed like a sailor. According to Hayden Herrera's *Frida: A Biography of Frida Kahlo*, those who knew her say that "she radiated a strange vitality that was a mixture of tenderness and willful spunk."

Those characteristics were evident throughout her life. When she met Rivera as a teenager, she snatched food from his lunch basket and soaped the stairs to see if he would fall. Once, while sharing ice cream with her prep school friends, she declared, "I will have Diego's baby just as soon as I convince him to cooperate."

The two painters were, in many ways, a perfect match. When asked to explain what drew them together, Frida said, "Diego was attracted to my mustache and I, to his breasts." He was fantastically fat and extravagant and created grand public art. She was petite and fierce and painted tiny pictures (most twelve by fifteen inches) in her home. She was a master of self-portraiture.

André Breton, the French poet and one of the founders of surrealism, once wrote, "There is no art more exclusively feminine, in the sense that, in order to be as seductive as possible, it is

> **No one is apart from anyone. No one fights for himself. All is all and one. Anguish and pain, pleasure and death are nothing but a process in order to exist.**

Previous pages: The painting *Me Twice* shows Kahlo as a 19th-century lady linked by an artery to herself dressed as an Indian. A surgeon's clip stops bleeding near her right hand to indicate she is childless. *Clockwise from top left:* Kahlo and Rivera receive Leon Trotsky and his wife in Tampico, Mexico; Kahlo, Rivera, and a pet monkey; Kahlo's studio and wheelchair at the Casa Azul museum in Mexico City; Kahlo in a hammock in the garden of Casa Azul in Coyoacán, Mexico, 1948; *Self-Portrait with Cropped Hair,* 1940, oil on canvas.

only too willing to play alternately at being absolutely pure and absolutely pernicious. That art of Frida Kahlo is a ribbon about a bomb."

Frida never competed with Rivera and insisted on forging her own identity. And Rivera admired strong women. He respected Frida for keeping her maiden name and for wanting to be financially independent. Perhaps as a symbolical gesture, he built two separate houses—one for her, and one for him—linked by a bridge to maintain this mutual autonomy. Rivera was one of her biggest supporters, often bragging that she was the only female Mexican painter to have conquered the Louvre.

In her youth, however, the woman whom Rivera dubbed the "best painter of the epoch" had no intentions of becoming an artist. She studied medicine at the National Preparatory School in Mexico City. She may have gravitated toward the medical field because of her own health issues: Tragically, at age six, she had been stricken with polio. But it was another blow that transpired on a rainy day in September 1925 that many art historians cite as a key turning point in her life. That fall day, a trolley rammed into a bus on which the teenage Frida was riding as a passenger.

"Before we had taken another bus," Frida wrote, "but since I had lost a little parasol, we got off to look for it and that was how we happened to get on the bus that destroyed me." The crash bounced her forward and a handrail literally skewered her body. Bizarrely, a painter on the same bus was carrying a packet of powdered gold. It exploded during impact, showering gold dust all over Frida's bleeding body. Later, a haunting sight confronted witnesses: a beautiful golden young woman sprawled on a table with blood gushing out of her. This poignant imagery foreshadowed what she would later represent in life: the heroic sufferer who transforms pain into something both precious and dazzling.

After the accident, doctors doubted that Frida would survive. Her spinal column was severed in three places. Her collarbone and ribs were broken. Her right thigh sustained eleven fractures; her right foot was both dislocated and crushed. Her shoulder was out of joint and her pelvis was smashed in three places. She had to wear various plaster corsets and learn to keep still. As part of her long recovery, Frida's mother asked a carpenter to make a special easel that would allow her to paint while lying down. Eventually, painting became essential to her well-being.

Frida's art—and personhood—were very much products of the time and place in which she lived. She was born in 1907 in the Mexico City suburb of Coyoacán, just three years before the outbreak of the Mexican Revolution. After a decade of struggle, Mexico was ready to turn away from European cultural and economic models and embrace its own native culture. Frida embodied this nationalistic fervor. Her lifelong passion for her cultural roots expressed itself in her dress, her home decor and, of course, in her art.

Her attire of choice was the traditional Tehuana costume—the kind one often sees in her paintings. Folklore has it that the indigenous women of Tehuantepec were stately, intelligent, brave, and sensuous. Through her dress, Frida linked herself to both this grand image of women and to Mexico's proud past. And she drew lots of attention parading the world's streets in her strikingly colorful outfits. (One story recounts that a group of young kids followed her down New York streets asking, "Where is the circus?")

Like her costumes, Mexico's popular art is full of festive colors: olive green, orange, purple, yellow, and red. Frida painted in this distinct palette as well, evoking an emotional tone both penetrating and intense.

She melded her love of both the traditional and the theatrical in everything she did. Yellow and blue walls lit by bare electric bulbs gave her home a flavor of the campesino culture. Lunchtime visitors, Herrera notes, would burst into fitful laughter as her pet parrot Bonito made his way around clay pots and Mexican platters on his tiny zygodactyl feet to get to his snack of choice—butter. Other friends recall hearing her other parrot, who regularly drank beer and tequila, curse and squawk, *No me pasa la cruda!* ("I can't get over this hangover!").

There was a sense of the fantastic in her work as well. Animals and nature figure prominently in Frida's art; a chipmunk might hug her profile lovingly in a self-portrait. In still lifes, she painted flowers and fruit from her own garden. But instead of placing these objects on a conventional tabletop, she set them against mountainous landscapes under glorious Mexican skies.

European art critics called her a surrealist because of these juxtapositions. But Frida said, "I don't know whether my paintings are surrealist or not, but I do know that they are the frankest expression of myself." Some critics now call her an extraordinary realist. Frida's images were not based on Freudian or philosophical theories. Rather, they came from her immediate experiences. She created a series of bloody and terrifying self-portraits—documenting her miscarriage in Detroit, the psychological wounds she endured from Rivera's infidelities, and the surgeries and plaster corsets that left her immobilized.

Remarkably, even her most painful self-portraits lack any sense of self-pity. Her desire to combat sadness was ferocious. Some recall that in her yearlong stay at the English Hospital, friends would visit and eat enchiladas and mole with her, enjoy the latest movies, which Rivera got for them, and relish the ever-present bottles of tequila. Confined to her hospital bed, Frida decorated her plaster casts with mirrors and feathers and performed toe-puppet shows for friends.

Throughout her life, Frida also passionately aligned herself with many social issues. While her mother was of Spanish and Mexican Indian descent, her father was a Hungarian-German Jew. Alarmed by Hitler's rise, Frida collected money to help refugees escape Nazi Germany. Once, when she and Rivera visited Detroit, they were shocked to learn that their hotel did not allow Jewish guests. They promptly told the owner that they had Jewish blood and planned to leave immediately. Desperate to keep the famous couple at his lodging, the owner offered to lower the rent. They stayed—but only on the condition that he remove the restriction altogether.

> I paint my own reality. The only thing I know is that I paint because I need to, and I paint whatever passes through my head without any other consideration.

Rivera and Frida also helped arrange for the departure of Loyalists suffering in the Spanish Civil War and donated their time and resources to their Communist activities. When the Russian revolutionary Leon Trotsky defected to Mexico, he lived in their home and was supported by them. It is also widely believed that the sensuous Frida had an affair with this legendary figure. But then she had numerous liaisons with both men and women.

Rivera's philandering only encouraged this behavior. But no matter how much she publicly laughed off Rivera's frequent escapades, Frida yearned for his love and attention. Grief-stricken and feeling betrayed after their divorce, in 1939, she cut off her hair and wore a man's suit for the revealing, iconic self-portrait she painted during this time.

Rivera could not live without Frida either. They remarried after the divorce but then led independent sexual lives. Rivera was unbothered by Frida's relationships with women; he even encouraged them. But when it came to other men, his sense of pride and machismo burned. The handsome American sculptor Isamu Noguchi recalled one particularly tense encounter with Rivera. Noguchi had come to the hospital to visit Frida one day and was confronted by Rivera pointing a gun at him. "Next time I see you, I'm going to shoot you," he told Noguchi. Rivera had discovered his affair with Frida and wanted him out of her life. A loaded gun did the trick.

The 1940s proved to be a fruitful decade for Frida. Her reputation as an artist grew both at home and abroad. She was included in major art exhibitions in Mexico and the U.S., and in 1942 she was selected as a founding member of the Seminario de Cultura Mexicana. This organization was made up of twenty-five artists and intellectuals whose mission was to promote the dissemination of Mexican culture through lectures and exhibitions. She received a government fellowship in 1946 and government commissions followed.

The art world's stars openly admired her work: Georgia O'Keeffe, Joan Miró, Yves Tanguy, and Pablo Picasso were all fans. Legend has it that once, as Picasso admired one of Frida's drawings, he turned to Rivera and said, "Neither you nor I are capable of drawing eyes like Frida!"

When the Lola Álvarez Bravo gallery presented Frida's work in a one-woman show in 1953, she considered it an important milestone in her career. It was Frida's first major solo exhibition in her native country. It took place just months before her death, in 1954, at the age of forty-seven. As the opening drew near, Frida's health was in a steady decline. Doctors forbade her to move, and it seemed she would not make it to her opening. But what transpired that evening has become part of the Frida legend.

The opening mirrored the true spirit of Frida and her art: colorful, morbid, theatrical, and emotional. There was a frenzy of excitement outside the gallery before the show. People pushed at the door to squeeze inside. Then, ambulance sirens sounded. Visitors stepped aside as Frida was wheeled into her exhibition—lying on a stretcher, impeccably dressed in her traditional costume, bedecked in jewelry, with her hair done up. She was slipped into her four-poster bed, which had been transferred earlier to the gallery. From there she held court while friends and fans took turns congratulating her. People gathered around singing Mexican ballads until well past midnight. As Herrera observed, "She may have been tired and broken, but she was bidding good-bye to life in her own gallant style."

A few months later, doctors amputated her right leg. Rivera recalls in his autobiography, *My Art, My Life*, published posthumously in 1960, that Frida became increasingly depressed after the surgery. One year later, on a cold and rainy July day, Frida disobeyed her doctor's orders and left her bed to participate in a Communist demonstration. Photographs of the protest show Rivera wheeling her alongside thousands of fellow Mexicans. She held a peace banner with an image of a dove in one hand. The other was adorned with rings and clenched in a fist. Following that protest rally, her pneumonia worsened and she became violently ill. She knew her life was fading. The night before she passed away, she gave Rivera the ring she had bought to celebrate their twenty-fifth anniversary, just seventeen days away. After her death, she was first laid to rest in her four-poster bed. Friends braided her hair with ribbons and flowers and dressed her in one of her traditional robes, placing rings on every finger.

Even fifty-seven years after her death, Frida Kahlo remains an inspiration. She was proud of her heritage and celebrated it—just as she celebrated herself. Unyieldingly determined to defeat sadness, she was, as Herrera so aptly writes, "the conquistador of happiness." She faced problems head-on, endured pain throughout her entire body, and yet remained faithful to the things that filled her life with joy. In the words of Carlos Fuentes, one of Mexico's greatest writers: "I think that Frida was a pantheist. I think Frida was in love with the world, with everything that was alive. Her love… appear[s] in her painting. She sort of sacrilizes the world."

Her final painting—completed only eight days before her death—is a testament to her spirit. In constant pain and confined to bed, she contemplated suicide. Instead, she chose joy. She dipped her brush in bloodred paint, and marked her farewell across the pulp of the watermelon still life before her. In large capital letters she painted the words VIVA LA VIDA!

Forugh
FARROKHZAD

(1935–1967)

The Poet and Her Poetry:
The Lover and the Beloved

By my bed stands a selection of family photographs, a simple book light, and a collection of works by Rumi, the famous thirteenth-century Persian poet. Granted, I don't read Persian well enough to fully grasp Rumi's verses in my native language, but even in their English translation his words are profound, life affirming, and deeply moving. They transcend national and ethnic borders.

It is no wonder that Iranians take special pride in their poets; lyric poetry is the country's highest and most revered art. My father's generation peppered its conversations with passages from the works of the classical Persian poets Rumi, Hafez, Sa'di, and Omar Khayyam. As children, we all worked hard to memorize and recite their poetry, both in school and at family gatherings. This deep love of Persian poetry followed me to the United States and sparked my nightly ritual of reading inspirational verses by my favorite poets.

One evening, I read the following passage from Rumi, which left me speechless:

> It is your turn now, you waited, you were patient.
>
> The time has come for us to polish you.
>
> We will transform your inner pearl into a house of fire.
>
> You're a gold mine, did you know that, hidden in the dirt of the earth?
>
> It is your turn now to be placed in fire.

I was hit by a wave of eerie energy. Just minutes earlier, I had been researching the life and poetry of Forugh Farrokhzad—Iran's most famous female poet. Now Rumi's words seemed to rise up from the annals of Persian history and call on this woman poet—some seven centuries later—to claim the stage.

In her tragically short thirty-two years on the planet, Forugh became a giant in Persian literature and changed the course of modern poetry. She was also well known as a filmmaker, an advocate for people suffering from leprosy, and a modern feminist—before that term was even commonly used in Iran. She surrendered herself to the "fire" of her art and paid a high price. But her struggles brought her ever closer to her calling.

Forugh's deference to her art recalls what the famed Sufi poets described as the quest of the lover for the beloved. "My lover is poetry," she once wrote. "I am going to seek my lover."

However, poetry seems to have beckoned Forugh as much as she pursued it. In the twenty-five hundred years since the beginning of recorded history in ancient Persia, much has been written about famous men and their accomplishments. Much less is known about the nation's women. "In the much revered classical period of Persian literature…not a single, significant woman poet or prose writer existed," notes Michael C. Hillman, a professor of Persian studies at the University of Texas–Austin, in *A Lonely Woman: Forugh Farrokhzad and Her Poetry.*

Hillman asserts that even educated Iranians cannot recall a woman by name from the Safavid (1501–1722) or Qajar (1796–1925) dynasties. This is because most Iranian women were restricted to the home, denied access to education, and had little opportunity for a public voice. Even generations later, very few women broke this ancestral silence because it meant challenging long-standing patriarchal, narrowly defined roles of femininity. According to Farzaneh Milani—a professor of Persian literature and cinema as well as women and Islam at the University of Virginia, past president of the Association of Middle Eastern Women Studies in America, and author of *Veils and Words*—women such as Forugh, who dared to "unveil their voices and expose their body of writing," suffered allegations of immorality, promiscuity, and even heresy.

It is within the confines of this social backdrop—working in a vacuum, without mentors or outside inspiration—that one should examine pioneering Iranian women such as Forugh who struggled to define themselves as creative individuals. As Hillman keenly notes, "Farrokhzad was more on her own in the mid-1950s than almost any woman writer from Europe or North America during the last two centuries." And yet she flourished. Writing from a singular feminine perspective, she published five poetry collections in her short lifetime, three before she turned twenty-four. With many reprints, her work has been among the most popular in modern Persian literature, but this feat is ever more surprising in light of her personal history.

Forugh was born in January 1935 to an authoritarian father, a career military officer, and a stern mother whose children knew her as "a slave to order, rules, and regulations." It may well have been this oppressive home environment that propelled Forugh to rebel. She was petite, attractive, inquisitive, and full of life. And by the time she reached her teen years, her independent spirit and interest in the opposite sex had become a concern for her parents.

At sixteen, she became enamored of a distant relative who was fifteen years her senior. Her parents caved in and allowed her to marry. Forugh's older sister, Puran, speculates that she was looking for a father figure who was kind and supportive—a man who would encourage her budding creative interests. And this was precisely the role that her husband, the noted satirist Parviz Shapour, played. Forugh began publishing stories and sketches in newspapers and magazines shortly after their marriage.

By the time she was twenty, Forugh published her first collection of poems, *Asir* (*The Captive*). But in those four years, her marriage had become strained. Forugh pursued a divorce—considered a reprehensible act for a woman at the time. As part of the divorce agreement, she had to relinquish custody of her beloved three-year-old son, Kamyar. (Prior to the 1967 Iranian Family Protection Act, children in divorce cases were routinely placed in the father's custody.) For the rest of her life, Forugh felt extreme guilt for having deprived her son of maternal love.

At the same time, though, she found solace in poetry's constant pull. As she writes in *The Captive*:

> I am that bird, that bird who for a long time
> has had thoughts in her head of flying. . .
> Come open the door so that
> I might spread my wings
> toward the bright sky of poetry.

Her frank, autobiographical voice in *The Captive* and her subsequent collections led to nothing short of public furor. It was a direct challenge to the traditionally guarded emotions of Iranian culture. At the same time, the sensual, erotic nature of her imagery, which employed feminine metaphors inspired by her own body and sensations, was deemed scandalous. Simply put, Forugh defied Iranian social mores and, as a result, scurrilous rumors were spread about her personal and romantic life. Several literary figures set out to defame her and asserted romantic relationships with her, which wounded her deeply.

Moreover, in the 1950s and '60s, the dominant force in the literary establishment was that of the traditionalist—a form of Persian poetry born in the ninth century that held sway for a millennium. In this school of poetry, verbal dexterity, verse form, and style were more prized than content, with praise and satire the most common attitudes. The romantic idyll was another major traditionalist form.

Forugh, in contrast, followed the pattern of the budding modernist movement, infusing modern subjects and images into conventional forms to express her individuality. For her, poetry had to reflect her everyday concerns and images: the home, the kitchen, visits to the bazaar, her grandmother's chador, sleeping outdoors on summer nights, New Year's preparations, the Iranian landscape, and, most significantly, her encounters with love. She used the colloquial language of everyday Persian, not the standard literary one. Some of her verses contain only a few syllables; others have twenty or more. Some are sentence fragments and some are run-ons. There are no expected end rhymes. To the traditionalists, modernist work such as Forugh's was a direct "rejection of the noblest art in Iranian history, a rejection of what, in other words, made Iranian culture particularly significant," Hillman writes.

With the publication of each new collection, Forugh's reputation as a poet grew, as did the many rumors and the negative criticism. But Forugh had resolved to live life and write poetry on her own terms; aspiring toward greater self-knowledge, she used poetry as a mirror.

"Her poetry is the chronicle of an evolving consciousness, the testament [of] a growing awareness," writes Milani. In fact, in Forugh's later collections, her range of symbolism and topics becomes more varied. For example, in her third collection, *Esian* (*Rebellion*), she combines Old Testament, Koranic, and traditional Persian literary poetry. In her later poems, she tackles such topics as social justice for the lower class, women's struggles, and Iran's blind surge toward modernization.

By her mid-twenties, Forugh had developed interests in cinematography, acting, and producing. At the time, Tehran was becoming the center of the most important indigenous cinema in the Middle East, and Forugh proved to be a significant figure in this field as well.

As a colleague, the Iranian theater director Pari Saberi, noted, "In the case of every art she confronted, she very quickly demonstrated that she had the capacity for that art, and she would fill herself with it and then produce." In 1958, Ebrahim Golestan, the famous Iranian writer and cinematographer, hired Forugh as an assistant at his film studio, and they soon became lovers.

It was not long before Forugh embarked on her own film projects. In the fall of 1962, she and three colleagues traveled to Tabriz and filmed *The House Is Black*—a documentary about a leper colony. The film's powerful imagery, touching narrative, and rhythmic, hypnotic cinematography earned it international acclaim and multiple prizes. For Forugh, *The House Is Black* was deeply satisfying not only professionally but also personally: Soon after the film was released, she adopted a boy from leper parents.

Forugh's repertoire was expanding ever more rapidly. She played a role in a 1963 Persian stage version of Luigi Pirandello's *Six Characters in Search of an Author* in Iran, and it was an unprecedented hit—largely because of her participation. The following year, her fourth book, *Tavalodi Digar* (*Another Birth*), exploded on the literary scene. Modernist critics immediately hailed it as a milestone of modern Persian poetry.

In the last year of her life, Forugh was very active, studying filmmaking and directing in London and participating in the second Pesaro Film Festival in Pesaro, Italy. However, a dark encounter marked this trip. She met an Italian gypsy who told her that a bloody accident was going to take place. Several months later, she and Golestan were injured in an accident while driving back from the Caspian Sea. But a bigger tragedy awaited her.

On February 14, 1967, after a visit to her mother's house, Forugh returned to Golestan's film studio. She then went out to pick up a reel of film. On the way back, she swerved her Jeep to avoid an oncoming vehicle and struck a wall. She died of head injuries before reaching the hospital.

The Tehran community's response was palpable; commemorative articles and eulogies flooded the press. Some called her the first female poet to have inaugurated a new chapter in Persian poetry. Even her critics hailed her as a remarkable artist. Her fifth collection of poetry, *Iman Biyavarim beh Aghaz-a Fasl-e Sard* (*Let Us Believe in the Dawning of a Cold Season*), was published posthumously, in 1974, yet another example of Forugh's legacy of fearless passion.

Golestan, the man who was closest to her, once likened Forugh to a bird—an image she used often in her poetry. With little guidance and surrounded by criticism, Forugh was nevertheless able to fly and soar, despite the inhospitable climate for independent-minded women at that time in Iran, when so few even risked flight. But she was willing to withstand criticism because of the pull of a stronger force—that of her quest for the beloved.

"Art is the strongest love," she once said. "It avails itself only to those who thoroughly surrender their whole existence to it." If art is the vehicle through which one achieves union with the beloved, then Forugh sought what the Sufis called her deeper self. Through the act of writing poetry, she discovered herself, and in her poems she craved understanding.

Page 77: Portrait of the poet.
Clockwise from top left:
Farrokhzad performs on stage in Tehran; portrait of the poet and filmmaker at work on the set of *The House Is Black*; Farrokhzad and her adopted son, Hossein Mansouri. She fell in love with him when she witnessed a teacher ask him for a beautiful phrase. His response? "Moon, sun, flower, game…" He is now a poet based in Berlin.

In the touching dedication of a poem to her son, Forugh once wrote:

> When your innocent eyes glance
>
> over this confused, beginningless book,
>
> you will see a deep-rooted lasting rebellion
>
> blooming in the heart of every song.

And then later:

> You will search for me in my words
>
> and tell yourself: My mother,
>
> that is who she was.

Perhaps Nasrin Rahimieh, a professor of comparative literature at the University of California–Irvine, and Dominic Parviz Brookshaw, a lecturer in Persian studies and Iranian literature at the University of Manchester, the editors of *Forugh Farrokhzad, Poet of Modern Iran*, summed it up best: "The difficult and painful choices she made as a young woman in search of her passions were not easily accepted by a society that expected women to confine themselves to being modest and self-sacrificing wives and mothers… She suffered publicly and privately. But she persevered and remained true to her own desire for different forms of self-fulfillment. As a result she left behind a remarkable legacy in her much-admired poems."

Farrokhzad has, arguably, become the most discussed Iranian woman in nearly three thousand years.

Golda MEIR

(1898–1978)

The Grandmother Diplomat

When you think about a female prime minister appearing in public, you probably imagine a well-coiffed, sophisticated woman in a tailored power suit. Her black pumps would be buffed, and her pocketbook would be discreet yet fashionable. Her mannerisms, too, would be very polished.

This was not Golda Meir. Golda was a frumpy, nicotine-stained grandmother who wore her hair in a low bun. She favored sensible orthopedic shoes and carried an old-fashioned handbag. She was unpackaged and seemingly ordinary, and this was perhaps her slickest political move of all: While the grandmother image won over hearts around the world, through it Golda Meir also projected a certain honesty, directness, and accessibility—and this is what Israel's formidable prime minister was all about.

Long before Margaret Thatcher, Benazir Bhutto, and Angela Merkel appeared on the global scene to lead the United Kingdom, Pakistan, and Germany, respectively, a spirited and determined Golda Meir carved out a role for herself in the male-dominated arena of international politics as a charismatic ambassador and a potent leader. A true anomaly in the corridors of power, Golda was a pioneer, serving as Israel's first female foreign minister, labor minister, and, of course, ultimately, as prime minister.

However, from the 1940s—before Israel's independence—until the 1970s, Golda was more than just a political figure: She personified the Israeli spirit. She was the international face and voice of the Jewish homeland in the Middle East at a time when the rest of the world was still forming its opinion of this nascent democracy.

I have had the pleasure of interviewing a number of people who knew her well, and their insights help paint a detailed picture of Golda's vibrant, multilayered personality. "When she

entered the room, everyone took notice," Yitzhak Navon, Israel's president from 1978 to 1983, told me. "There was no pretension. When she spoke, everyone would listen. She was sure of herself and convincing. Her ideals came from the bottom of her heart."

"She had a range of personalities," said Rebecka Belldegrun, a close family friend who knew Golda from a young age and who later made her the godmother of her son. "One minute she was brilliant, sharp, almost masculine. Then there was the complete transformation where she became a grandmother, easily tearful and feminine."

Golda was born in Kiev, Russia (now the capital of Ukraine) in 1898, but her family moved to the United States when she was a child to escape brutal pogroms. The helplessness that she saw in her father during these anti-Semitic attacks stayed with her throughout her life. "To this day I remember how scared I was and how angry I was that all my father could do to protect me was to nail a few planks together while we waited for the hooligans to come," she wrote in her 1975 autobiography, *My Life*.

> It's no accident many accuse me of conducting public
> affairs with my heart instead of my head. Well,
> what if I do? Those who don't know how to weep with
> their whole heart don't know how to laugh either.

When the family settled in Wisconsin, her father, Moshe, worked in the railroad yards of Milwaukee while her mother, Bluma, worked in a grocery store. Golda attended public schools—including one that would later be named after her. From an early age she displayed strong leadership skills, such as organizing a school fund-raiser for textbooks. Her goal was to finish school and become a teacher, but her parents had other plans. Golda was still in high school when Bluma announced that she had found the perfect husband for her.

After several heated rows, the independent-minded Golda ran away to live with an older sister and brother-in-law in Denver. There she embraced Zionism, a topic often discussed in her sister's household, and met Morris Myerson, a Russian émigré who would later become her husband. Golda and Morris moved back to Milwaukee so she could attend high school and later college. But soon Zionism began to consume Golda's every waking moment. She had found her calling, and, more than anything, she wanted to help build a Jewish state.

By 1921 she was able to convince Morris to join her in leaving the United States to live in her "dreamland." After fifty-three days of exhausting travel, the married couple finally stepped off a train in Tel Aviv and looked around. Alas, it was not what she expected!

There were flies everywhere, some carrying malaria. The stench of donkeys was overpowering, as were the open latrines. But there was no turning back. Golda and Morris joined a kibbutz, where work began each morning at 4:00 a.m. before the flies and heat became unbearable. (Local Arabs called the Jezreel Valley, the area where the kibbutz was located, the Death Swamp.) There was also no privacy for the couple. Life on a kibbutz meant communal living—a communal dining room, toilets, showers—and sleeping arrangements. In my interview, the former Israeli president Navon noted the marked contrast in her new surroundings: "Here was a woman from Milwaukee who joined a kibbutz. There was nothing so opposite to the American capitalistic view."

Nevertheless, Golda thrived. She became the kibbutz's representative to the Histadrut (General Federation of Labor). After moving with her husband to Jerusalem, where she gave birth to two children, and then to Tel Aviv a few years later, she became secretary of that organization's women's labor council and eventually a member of its executive committee, which helped foster relations between the burgeoning Jewish homeland and the United States. In these posts, she had opportunities to hone her growing powers of political persuasion.

Not long after, she proved herself to be a magnetic and wildly successful fund-raiser for Israel at a time of critical importance. During the forties, Golda returned to the United States to raise money. She dazzled audiences with her idealism and emotional pleas, collecting an astounding $50 million on her first tour (local Israeli leaders had initially hoped for $7 million).

When the state of Israel was established, in 1948—Golda was among those who signed the country's founding declaration—she rose quickly, accepting the post of ambassador to Moscow that same year, and then served as minister of labor from 1949 to 1956, and as foreign minister from 1956 to 1966. Part of her appeal was, without a doubt, the fact that she seemed to resemble everyone's grandmother. Her "ordinary" demeanor—she smoked Chesterfield cigarettes and still mopped her own floors—was endearing, yet she always held her own with the leading international political figures of the time. "Not being beautiful forced me to develop my inner resources," she once said.

According to Elinor Burkett, author of the 2008 biography *Golda*, the doors to her home were always open, to both personal and political visitors; in fact, her kitchen was once dubbed an "Israeli political institution." In one particularly striking story, Frank Church, the influential U.S. senator from Idaho, came to visit her at home in Israel, and Golda promptly disappeared. Not sure what she was up to, Church went to find her.

"You came to help?" Golda asked, as he appeared in the kitchen.

"Okay, why not?" he replied.

"No. Go into the living room and I'll bring you breakfast," she said. Then she added, "But there are a few things you can help me with—Phantoms, land-to-air missiles, and help Russian

Jews to emigrate." In this way, the inimitable Golda forged personal connections with leaders the world over, embracing a direct, intimate approach that surprised many and often trumped the more formal, standard dignitary meeting. "If only political leaders would allow themselves to feel as well as to think, the world might be a happier place," she once said.

And political leaders across the globe adored her. The former American president Richard Nixon loved her, although she lectured him relentlessly. He once announced in the Knesset (Israel's parliament) that there was no leader with "greater courage, greater intelligence, and greater stamina, greater determination, and greater dedication to her country than Prime Minister Meir."

Trust yourself. Create the kind of self that you will be happy to live with all your life. Make the most of yourself by fanning the tiny, inner sparks of possibility into flames of achievement.

Golda's charm was also evident in her relationship with one particular Arab leader. In 1947, she slipped across the border to conduct secret negotiations with Jordan's King Abdullah. The king had been told he was to meet the second most important Zionist diplomat and was shocked to encounter a woman. But over the years, they became unlikely friends. Later, on the occasion of her seventy-fifth birthday, the king's grandson, King Hussein, gave her an exquisite strand of pearls, considered to be "stones of paradise" in the Koran.

Golda earned great respect for her work. As the country built its infrastructure, she proved to be a pivotal figure in negotiating labor disputes, enabling the construction of a staggering thirty thousand houses when she was minister of labor, and finding ways to integrate the thousands of immigrants seeking haven from war-torn Europe. Burkett notes that Golda also became a familiar figure across Africa as she forged bonds with the newly emerging African states. Later, she took on the unenviable task of battling the outsize egos in the splintered political parties within her own country.

She was also known for her stamina. Once, according to Belldegrun, in Finland, Golda announced that she would not sleep until the sun went down. It was the time of year, however, when Finland boasts a midnight sun—so when her security guards became tired, she told them to go to bed while she sat up late into the night, smoking cigarettes.

In her later years, Golda suffered from migraines, heart trouble, kidney stones, and lymphoma. The prime minister was not one to complain, though, and went straight from her morning rounds of cancer treatment at Israel's Hadassah University Medical Center to work to conduct government business.

"How's your health?" a journalist once asked. "Nothing serious," she replied. "A touch of cancer here… a little tuberculosis there." Yet she still managed to keep up with her male colleagues—even those who were much younger.

Her self-assurance made her an intimidating leader. "I swear she grows an inch every time she walks through the door," a government minister once told *Newsweek*. But this same quality sometimes worked against her. She was known to be intolerant of differing opinions, and, as a younger generation of Israeli leaders came up through the ranks, some perceived her as uncompromising and out-of-date.

> Only those who dare, who have the courage
> to dream, can really accomplish something. People
> who are forever asking themselves, "Is it realistic?
> Can it be accomplished? Is it worth trying?"
> accomplish nothing…. What's realistic? A stone?
> Something that's already in existence?
> That's not realism. That's death.

At seventy-five, Golda was at the peak of her popularity as prime minister when disaster hit. In October 1973, Egypt and Syria launched an overwhelming surprise attack that began on Yom Kippur, the holiest day of the Jewish calendar. Prior to the war, Israeli intelligence reports had discovered a surge of Egyptian troops along the Suez Canal, yet despite this ominous assembly, Golda reluctantly sided with Israel's defense minister, Moshe Dayan, who wanted to delay mobilizing Israeli forces and refrain from launching a preemptive strike. Israel paid a heavy price in casualties for being unprepared, and many blamed Golda. Drawing on her research, Burkett asserts that during the darkest days of the war, when Dayan was in despair and contemplating surrender, it was Golda who refused to buckle under pressure. In fact, she helped lead Israel to regain its position. An independent Israeli commission appointed after the war exonerated Golda. Nonetheless, she never regained the popularity she had before the war.

One of her great disappointments, of course, was her inability to forge true peace with Egypt during her tenure. Navon recalls visiting a ruminative Golda in the hospital toward the

66 66 Ability hits the mark
where presumption
overshoots and
diffidence falls short. 99

Page 83: Israeli guard of honor welcomes Meir at Sharm El Sheik during her visit to the Sinai front, 1970. *Previous pages:* The U.S. President and Mrs. Nixon with Meir, 1973. *From top:* U.S. Secretary of State Henry Kissinger shakes hands with Meir, 1974; Meir, Moshe Sharett, and others at the signing of the Israeli Declaration of Independence at the Tel Aviv Museum, May 14, 1948; Meir visits Sinai, 1970; Golda Meir smoking, at Kibbutz Revivim in 1973, courtesy of GadCollection.

end of her life. "She was bitter," he said, explaining that Golda was upset with her critics. He recalled her queries: "That's what they accused me of? That I spoiled the possibility of peace?"

Indeed, during her tenure as prime minister she had tried on different levels, albeit unsuccessfully, to forge a lasting peace treaty through direct negotiations. When the Egyptian president Anwar el-Sadat finally came to Israel for peace talks during Menachem Begin's term as prime minister, he took Golda's hand and said, "Madam, for many, many years I wanted to meet you." Her response: "Mr. President… Why didn't you come earlier?" Sadat paused. "The time was not yet ripe," he replied.

Golda Meir died on December 8, 1978, in Jerusalem—just two days before Sadat and Begin were awarded the Nobel Peace Prize. A generation later, the world continues to celebrate her as a pioneering nation builder, a respected and effective diplomat, and a charismatic leader who epitomized what one woman can accomplish on the world stage.

Rigoberta
MENCHÚ TUM

(1959–)

The Symbolic Storyteller

An unassuming-looking woman sits with her hands clasped on her lap. Against a dark background, her face is bright, round, and youthful. She wears a traditional multicolored *huipil* and a skirt. Then she opens her mouth; she is a natural-born storyteller. She recites this poem in a soft, gentle voice:

> *I crossed the border, love. I will return tomorrow*
> *when tortured Mama weaves another colorful blouse,*
> *when Papa, burned alive, he awakens to greet the sun*
> *from the four corners of our little hut.*
> *There will be drink for all. There will be incense,*
> *the laughter of little children and joyful embraces.*

This is Rigoberta Menchú Tum, Guatemala's famed human rights advocate, in just one of many mesmerizing scenes she commands in the tragic documentary *When the Mountains Tremble*. The 1983 Sundance Film Festival Special Jury Award–winning film offers a glimpse into the struggles of a peaceful Guatemalan Mayan Indian population struck down by an oppressive government, as represented by Rigoberta's own astonishing personal story. A member of the Quiché Mayan tribe, Rigoberta was a mere twenty-one years old at the time of filming, but as she intimates in her poem, she had already experienced and witnessed more than a lifetime's worth of atrocities: A younger brother and both parents were tortured and killed by the Guatemalan armed forces, and she had been forced into exile after repeated death threats.

Elisabeth Burgos-Debray—who worked closely with Rigoberta on the recording and translation of her history for the book *I, Rigoberta Menchú: An Indian Woman in Guatemala*— writes in its introduction that Rigoberta "speaks for all the Indians of the American continent…

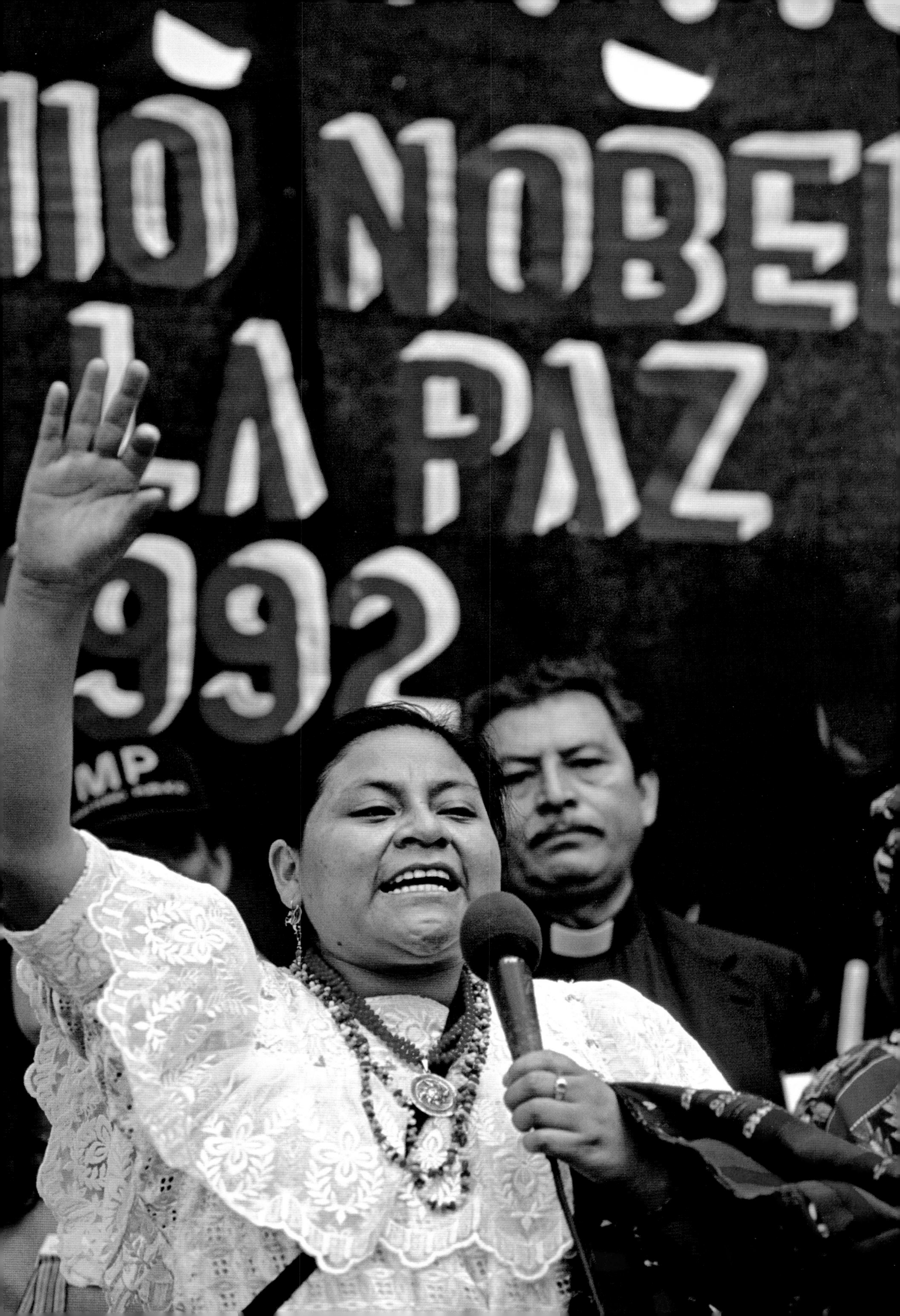
LA PAZ
MP

The cultural discrimination she has suffered is something that all the continent's Indians have been suffering ever since the Spanish conquest." What sets Rigoberta's story apart, however, is that she demanded a voice for both herself and her people. She put a human face on the suffering of thousands, and she dedicated her life to fighting for respect and fair treatment for her people.

According to her autobiography, Rigoberta was born in 1959 in the tangle of unfertile mountains in the Altiplano, or high plateau, of Guatemala. In the 1960s, her family began cultivating the land, but it barely sustained them. So members of her family and the surrounding community would travel to the southern coast for months at a time to work on fincas, or farms, to pick coffee and cotton for little pay and meager food.

A wealthy mixed-race minority known as Ladinos, who were themselves backed by the ruling military officers, owned the fincas. Living conditions on the fincas were horrendous: Workers were provided with very little food, and four to five hundred people—workers and their children—were housed in a *galera*, a wall-less structure with a palm- or a banana-leaf thatched roof. According to Rigoberta, two of her brothers died on the fincas: Felipe, the eldest, whom she never knew, of pesticide intoxication; Nicolas, the youngest, of malnutrition.

Rigoberta writes that her mother, a healer and a midwife, also worked on a finca until a month before she was born and that her mother went up into the mountains to give birth to her, the sixth child, on her own.

Rigoberta's father and mentor, Vicente, was a day laborer and a representative of their community, and Rigoberta—his favorite daughter—often accompanied him to the city on community business. He taught her about the ongoing conflicts between the Ladino landowners and her people. The Mayan Indians believed the Altiplano was rightfully theirs; the Ladinos also made claims on the property and repeatedly tried to drive the tribes off the land.

This conflict steadily escalated over the years. According to *I, Rigoberta Menchú*, in 1967, the army began repeatedly raiding the Quiché Mayan tribe's homes and kidnapped, tortured, and killed activists. Rigoberta's father was himself taken and abused. The Mayan Indian community, in turn, organized. Members began building their homes closer together so they could more easily alert one another about raids. They prepared traps on the main paths leading to the village and dug large ditches and underground paths. Women and men took turns keeping watch. By 1977, Vicente had joined the Peasant Unity Committee (CUC), which was dedicated to achieving fair treatment and wages from landowners and building respect for the Mayan Indian religion and culture. Soon, the CUC began organizing strikes and demonstrations.

The role that Guatemalan women played in their country's resistance movement is especially unique. Indeed, in her book, Rigoberta summed up her own mother's ideas: "Any evolution, any change, in which women had not participated, would not be a change, and there would be no victory." Both parents encouraged their young daughter to become a leader and an organizer.

Born into the great tradition of oral histories, Rigoberta was raised in a community that valued storytelling as a way to preserve vital cultural and ancestral information. Her rhetorical talents were also cultivated by her Catholic faith. Rigoberta studied and preached the Bible from an early age and embraced its stories of triumph in the face of seemingly overwhelming adversity: the life of Moses, who freed his people from bondage; and David, the poor young shepherd who defeated the mighty giant Goliath.

> My life does not belong to me. I've decided
> to offer it to a cause. They can kill me at any time,
> but let it be when I am fulfilling a mission.

Armed with such stories, the young Rigoberta moved from village to village, harnessing the power of words to educate and inspire. However, she quickly recognized that a tremendous barrier existed, as each of the twenty-two Guatemalan indigenous groups speaks its own language. So she learned Mam, Cakchiquel, Tzutujil, and Spanish—"the language of her oppressors," in the words of Burgos-Debray—to better communicate with the various tribes and those in power. With these skills, she taught men, women, and children how to organize and defend themselves.

By 1979, Rigoberta had joined the CUC. That September, her sixteen-year-old brother, the secretary of her community, was kidnapped, tortured, and murdered. Shortly after, tragedy struck again. In an effort to call international attention to their cause, in early 1980, her father and several other freedom fighters took over Guatemala City's Spanish embassy. The Guatemalan National Police set fire to the building, burning thirty-nine people alive, including Vicente.

Reaction to the tragedy was strong. Spain broke off all relations with Guatemala. Rigoberta, devastated, became increasingly active in the CUC. In 1980, she played an important role in a strike the CUC organized to improve conditions for farm workers on the Pacific coast. But only months after her father's death, Rigoberta's mother, who was also active in organizing and representing the CUC, was herself raped, tortured, and killed. A heartbroken Rigoberta fled to Mexico in 1981, where she found refuge with members of a liberal Roman Catholic group and began an international campaign to call attention to the plight of the Guatemalan Mayan Indians.

In 1982, while in Paris promoting her cause, Rigoberta dictated her story to Elisabeth Burgos-Debray. *I, Rigoberta Menchú*'s impact was extraordinary, bringing worldwide attention to the Guatemalan Mayan Indians' plight and making Rigoberta the face of the struggle. Her impassioned activism so captivated the international community that she was nominated for and awarded the Nobel Peace Prize in 1992, at just thirty-three, making her the first indigenous person and the youngest person ever to receive the honor. Indeed, the Nobel Prize accorded to Rigoberta was, in her words, a "symbolic recognition of the victims of repression, racism and poverty, as well as an homage to indigenous women."

The honor helped Rigoberta's cause. In 1993 she played a key role in bringing the human rights activist Ramiro de León Carpio to power as president. In 1996 the Guatemalan government and the rebel leaders signed a cease-fire, which put an end to Latin America's longest civil war— thirty-six years of conflict. The agreements included the resettlement and economic integration of displaced people, the establishment of a human rights commission, and recognition of cultural diversity and the right of indigenous people to practice their own cultural norms.

Much controversy has surrounded Rigoberta's life story, as documented in *I, Rigoberta Menchú*. In 1998, the anthropologist David Stoll asserted that Rigoberta had distorted key facts in her autobiography, among them, that her family was not as poor as she had depicted, and that although her brother was killed, he was not burned to death in front of the townspeople. Stoll also disputed her account of her education. Nevertheless, Stoll conceded that Rigoberta was invaluable in telling a story that "enabled her to focus international condemnation on an institution that deserved it, the Guatemalan army."

Rigoberta went on to receive fourteen honorary doctorates. She has also been a UNESCO Goodwill Ambassador since 1996 and was awarded the prestigious Prince of Asturias Award for International Cooperation in 1998. In 2004, she accepted President Óscar Berger's offer to help implement the Guatemalan peace accords. She ran, although unsuccessfully, in 2007, for the presidency of Guatemala. Throughout her very public life, she has put her international clout to good use. When prosecutions of crimes of genocide and torture committed by the military establishment led nowhere in Guatemala, she campaigned to have key members tried in Spanish courts. More recently, in 2006, she cofounded the Nobel Women's Initiative along with her fellow female laureates Jody Williams, Shirin Ebadi, Wangari Maathai, Betty Williams, and Máiread Corrigan Maguire. These six women represent North and South America, Africa, the Middle East, and Europe, and the initiative's mission is "to help strengthen work being done in support of women's rights around the world."

Very few indigenous Mayan Indian women have ever been in the world spotlight; Rigoberta's commitment to using her life story and popularity for the good of the many is indeed remarkable. There is no doubt that the support of her family and her resilient personality played a role in making her the leader that she is. But Rigoberta also credits the richness of her cultural upbringing and the universal messages embedded in her country's traditional rituals as a much-needed source of wisdom for her trials and tribulations.

Page 91: Menchú Tum, winner of the 1992 Nobel Peace Prize. ***Clockwise from top left:*** President Morales and Menchú Tum wave to supporters in Sucre, 2006; Menchú Tum kneels at a ceremony in commemoration of genocide victims in Guatemala, 2006; Menchú Tum and Bolivia's President Evo Morales join shamans in a ritual in Tiawanacu.

> I didn't learn my politics at school.
> I just tried to turn my own experience
> into something which was common
> to a whole people.

Over the years, Rigoberta has consistently called attention to the deeper messages in the *despedida,* a traditional Guatemalan farewell ceremony for newly married women. When a bride leaves her parents' home to enter the home of her husband's family, she is asked to walk out of the house without turning back. This act signifies an important lesson that the bride takes into her new life. As Rigoberta wrote in *I, Rigoberta Menchú,* her parents said of her sister: "She must not look back when she's faced with all the problems she will meet. She must always go forward."

Rigoberta has taken this traditional message to heart. Her ability to move forward despite great hardship has marked her personal journey—and her fight for the rights of her people. Her defiance has always been—and continues to be—rooted in positive universal values. Upon meeting her in Los Angeles in 2008, I was struck by how tranquil and delicate the then forty-nine-year-old national heroine was: Despite, or perhaps because of, everything she had seen and experienced, she was still very much the young woman from the 1983 documentary. Her optimism was undaunted. As she wrote in her autobiography: "I have faith and I believe that happiness belongs to everyone."

Nawal
EL MOUTAWAKEL

(1962–)

"The Black Gazelle"

There is a famous Moroccan saying that's been around for decades: "Never run when you can walk." But if Nawal El Moutawakel had seriously followed this popular proverb, she would never have become the first African-born Muslim woman to earn an Olympic gold medal.

As a matter of fact, all she did was run. As a young girl, she ran barefoot through the streets of Casablanca; she raced her brother along the beach and beat the boys in the track club in her hometown. After she raced to the finish line at the 1984 Olympic Games, in Los Angeles, she ran a victory lap carrying a Moroccan flag. In that instant, she became an icon for Muslim women athletes—as well as a national heroine. The king of Morocco called to personally congratulate her and proclaimed that all girls born on the day of the victory would be named Nawal, which means "gift of god."

I remember the '84 Olympic Summer Games in my beloved city of Los Angeles very clearly. The town was packed with tourists from all over the world wearing T-shirts bearing the Olympic logo of blue, white, and red stars. The University of California–Los Angeles was the host of the Olympic Village and the gymnastic games. While my friends and I walked around the college campus or through nearby Westwood Village, Olympic visitors would often stop us to ask for directions.

I also remember seeing Nawal's famous race on television. Her victory in Los Angeles was completely unexpected. Before the match, a fellow competitor bent down to give her a hug. At five-feet-two-inches tall and weighing just over one hundred pounds, she was quite the petite track star. Nawal later recalled that before the race she was suffering from both an upset stomach and a sore ankle. But once she hit her mark, all that was forgotten. The four-hundred-meter hurdles race has been referred to as "a gut-wrenching test of speed and strength with ten barriers thrown in." That August day, her performance was flawless. Her fast, graceful, rhythmic running and jumping at the games earned her the nickname the Black Gazelle.

"My athletic race was the four-hundred-meter hurdles, but it has been a metaphor for my life," Nawal once said. "It has been up and down; there are sometimes obstacles in the way. You have to get over the hurdles and keep running." Video clips of Nawal's victory lap reveal tears running down her face.

Nawal was born in 1962 in Casablanca, Morocco, in an era where the odds were certainly against her. It is unusual for Muslim women in the developing world to dedicate their time and resources to sports—much less to hurdles or running. But Morocco, which won its independence from France in 1956, is considered a liberal Muslim country. King Hassan II, who ruled from 1961 to 1999, was a progressive thinker and led his country toward modernization while maintaining religious and cultural traditions. Nawal's father also adhered to this progressive ideology. He was the one who first encouraged her to run. When she practiced at the track club in Casablanca, her father let her skip chores at home so she could concentrate on studying and running.

"My mother and father let me do what I wanted to do," she once told the *Chicago Tribune*'s Phil Hersh. She added, "We could have had many great female athletes in Morocco if the environment let them. Most start at thirteen and step out of sport at eighteen because they are told it is not something for girls to keep doing."

Her parents took exception to this rule. One day, Jean-François Coquand, a French coach studying Arabic in Morocco, spotted Nawal on the track and gave her tips on how to lengthen her stride and improve her running posture. She committed to hours of practice and training with Coquand, and by 1982, she had become the African champion in the one-hundred-meter high hurdles. Encouraged by her achievement, her father told her, "Train to be [an] Olympic champion… Aim far and high." And that she did.

Coquand had suggested that Nawal's natural skills were a good match for the new four-hundred-meter intermediates. (Before the 1983 IAAF World Championships, no such race had taken place.) She placed twenty-sixth in the '83 world championships, but a fortuitous meeting happened at that event. Nawal met Sunday Uti, a Nigerian quarter-miler who was attending school at Iowa State University. He was impressed with her talent and raved about her to his coaches at the college.

Nawal told Hersh that when the applications from Iowa State University arrived at her house, her first inclination was to put them aside. For one thing, she couldn't read a word of English. But most importantly, she had dismissed any hope that her father would ever agree to send her to a foreign country. Despite her qualms, she finally got up the courage to share the news with him.

> **I have the satisfaction of contributing to the liberation of Muslim women—or, rather, of Muslim men, who will have been forced to meditate on my ability.**

Previous pages: El Moutawakel takes her victory lap at the Los Angeles Olympics, 1984. *From top:* El Moutawakel receives her gold medal; El Moutawakel races during a visit with the Laureus Peace Players Project in Durban, South Africa, 2010; Brazilian soccer legend Pelé and El Moutawakel play during an inspection visit in Rio de Janeiro, 2009; French president Jacques Chirac welcomes IOC inspection committee member El Moutawakel at the Élysée Palace, Paris, 2005; a Run for Life race, 2007.

"I will think it over," Mohamed told his daughter. But it took him only twenty seconds to hurry after Nawal and announce, "I have thought it over. You will go." Some of Nawal's family members shook their heads in disbelief. Send a daughter to a foreign land to study and run? That was not the normal life story of a Moroccan girl!

My athletic race was the four-hundred-meter hurdles, but it has been a metaphor for my life. It has been up and down; there are sometimes obstacles in the way. You have to get over the hurdles and keep running.

But in the winter of 1984, Nawal left Casablanca for the cornfields of Iowa. Her first months in America were utterly dreadful. She spoke very little English and was terribly homesick. When her coaches at Iowa State asked her to run two hundred meters, she ran those—and then kept running until she finished five hundred meters. She had no idea what the coaches were saying. All she could do was muster a smile. As she recalls, she wore that nervous smile quite often on campus. But just weeks into her college stay, Nawal received devastating news: Her adoring father, her mentor, had died.

Grief-stricken, angry, and alone, she channeled all her energy into running. She broke collegiate records and lost only one four-hundred-meter hurdles race. That same year, she was invited to compete with the Moroccan track team at the Olympics in Los Angeles. She quickly agreed.

Her country soon pinned its hopes on this petite powerhouse—and she triumphed. Nawal attributes her success to another famous French saying, one her father used to tell her often: *Les chiens aboient, et la caravane passe.* ("The dogs bark, and the caravan passes.") This maxim highlights the importance of pressing on and ignoring the naysayers. Without the support of a single female coach, trainer, or other teammate, Nawal still emerged as a leading athlete, not only in her own country but also on the entire African continent.

Nawal's unexpected victory sparked celebrations all over Morocco. When she returned, Nawal and Said Aouita, Morocco's other gold medalist, rode with King Hassan II and Princess Lalla Meryem in a homecoming victory parade. Close to a million jubilant Moroccans lined the streets, chanting and cheering.

In some ways, the floodgates of change for African women burst open with Nawal's achievement. Congratulatory statements appeared in newspapers across Morocco and neighboring countries. "I hope your victory will give birth to a new generation of women who are not only our mothers, sisters, and wives, but our equals in adversity as well as triumph," wrote Aziz Mahoub in *Young Africa* magazine. Indeed, Nawal has used her status and skills to help bring about this kind of change. "I have the satisfaction of contributing to the liberation of Muslim women—or, rather, of Muslim men, who will have been forced to meditate on my ability," she said.

And while Nawal is certainly proud of her gold medal, it has not been the ultimate prize for her. In the seventeen years since she became an Olympic champion, she has gone on to hold many important posts. In 1998, she became a member of the prestigious International Olympic Committee. Nawal also chaired the IOC's evaluation commission for host city selection for the 2012 Summer Games, which made her the highest-ranking female on the committee. She is the only Olympic committee member who has been appointed as the minister of youth and sports in Morocco. In 2008–09, she served as the chairperson of the IOC's evaluation commission of the 2016 Olympic Games, and since 2010 she has served as chairperson of the coordination commission for the 2016 Olympic Games in Rio de Janeiro.

Nawal has been the recipient of many honors and accolades. She was awarded the National Merit (Exceptional Order) by King Hassan II of Morocco in 1983. And King Mohammed VI of Morocco awarded her the Mérite National de l'Ordre de Commandeur in 2004. Two years later, she was inducted into the Women's Sports Foundation's International Women's Sports Hall of Fame. And in 2010, Nawal received the Lifetime Achievement Award from the Laureus association.

Nawal's philosophy is that athletics can become a powerful agent for change. This Olympic legend has encouraged women's participation in sports by founding the Courir pour le Plaisir ("Run for Fun"), a ten-kilometer (6.2 miles) run in her homeland. In 2006, a record twenty-five thousand women, ages fifteen to seventy-five, ran through the streets of Casablanca to take part in it.

Nowadays, Nawal has also taken on the same important role that her beloved father once played in her earlier life—that of a mentor who recognizes and develops talent, and enables others to become more than they previously thought possible. "If we can break the mold that inhibits so many young people, we can make a profound change both in my country and around the world. It's not a revolution; it's a celebration," she says.

And so Nawal keeps celebrating with women all over world, especially in other Muslim countries. With an infectious smile and boundless enthusiasm, she recently told an audience in Abu Dhabi, "The future of sports belongs to the feminine."

Nawal now lives in Morocco with her husband, Mounir Bennis, and their two children.

She remains a woman who is more apt to run than walk.

Anaïs NIN

(1903–1977)

Writer, Dreamer, Temptress

Reading someone's diary is, by definition, a very intimate affair. But reading the diary of a well-known feminist—especially the first prominent woman to be known for her erotica—can be downright exotic. Such is the case with the journals of Anaïs Nin, the brilliant author, dreamer, and temptress whose deeply personal writings, penned over half a century, continue to captivate and inspire women across the globe.

For Nin, writing about her deepest desires became a source of personal liberation. Her diaries are bold and remarkably insightful. Years after their publication, the diaries, along with her other published literary works—and details about her intriguing love affairs and now-famous bigamous marriage—still fascinate the world.

The first day I ventured out to study her original manuscripts, I had the giddy feeling of being drawn toward a secret treasure. When I entered the special collections section of the Charles E. Young Research Library at the University of California–Los Angeles, I felt I'd landed in a wonderland. Glass cabinets encasing rare, leather-bound books stood against the perimeter walls. In no time, the librarian carried in six volumes of Anaïs Nin's original diaries in her cloth-gloved hands. The journals are rather dainty, with gold trim and gold-edged paper. I picked up a blue one first. Inside its cover she had written:

Mon Journal and Notebooks

(The numeral forty-one was crossed out and the numeral forty-two was written instead.)

Anaïs Nin's secret diaries were not published until 1966. At the time, the countercultural revolution was in full swing, and feminism was gaining wider acceptance. Soon after the publication of her diaries, Nin joined the growing ranks of female role models who were changing the way the world thought about women.

In many ways, her life was a series of transformations. "We travel, some of us forever, to seek other states, other lives, other souls," she wrote. She had an uncanny ability to connect her deepest desires, which sprung from the subterranean world of her unconscious, to her daily life. She was a flamenco dancer, a lay analyst, a writer, a wife, a lover, and a supporter of many of her era's most famous literary and artistic talents.

Anaïs began documenting her life in diaries at the age of eleven and didn't stop until her death, in 1977. In all, she penned sixty-nine volumes of elegant prose. These journals were her most prized possessions, and she stored them in bank vaults. Once asked why she had such an attachment to them, her response was swift: "Mine is the story of the soul, of the inner life… It is the study of the human heart seeking to express itself in life."

Today her journals are considered classic examples of modern feminist writing, largely because of her frankness and emotional and psychological intensity. As Deirdre Bair, the author of the 1995 biography *Anaïs Nin*, notes, "The twentieth century will be remembered for many concepts that brought sweeping societal change, and Anaïs Nin was among the pioneers who explored three of the most important: sex, the self, and psychoanalysis."

Anaïs once wrote, "Throw your dreams into space like a kite, and you do not know what it will bring back, a new life, a new friend, a new love, a new country." She had the courage to dream, and new beginnings, new loves, and new countries awaited her. The many names given to her at birth seem to have foreshadowed the multifaceted life she would live. Her full name was Angela Anaïs Juana Antolina Rosa Edelmira Nin y Culmell, which was shortened to Anaïs Nin. She was born in 1903 in Paris shortly after her parents had married and relocated from Cuba. She was of mixed descent—Spanish, Cuban, French, and Danish. Anaïs never fully identified with one language or with one specific culture or country. Her life reflected the same pattern; she lived in cities across the globe, including Paris, Brussels, Barcelona, New York, and Los Angeles.

She inherited an artistic sensibility from both parents. Her mother, Rosa, was a classical singer; her father, Joaquin, a pianist and a composer. Joaquin was a narcissist and a womanizer, who was more often than not on tour away from home. He had terrible bouts of rage during which he would beat or sexually abuse little Anaïs. This behavior left its mark on his daughter, and throughout her life she wrote about this complicated father-daughter relationship.

Anaïs was eleven when Joaquin abandoned the family for good. Rosa, in need of support, took Anaïs and her two brothers to live with Joaquin's parents in Barcelona. But shortly afterward, Rosa decided to move to New York to be close to her own sister. Around this time, Rosa bought a journal for her young daughter. She worried about the increasingly introverted Anaïs and thought writing might distract her from the stress of abandonment and relocation. Anaïs's first diary began as a letter to her father—a simple way to commit to paper her deep wish to woo him back.

> **Eroticism is one of the basic means of self-knowledge, as indispensable as poetry.**

Previous pages: Portrait of Anaïs Nin. *From left*: Nin as a Spanish dancer in Paris, under the name Anita Guilera; two of Nin's legendary publications, *Delta of Venus* and *The Early Diary of Anaïs Nin: Volume 2, 1920–1923.*

On page seventy-five of her forty-second journal (the first I read), she wrote: "I realized how this mask (father's mask) terrorized me. The tense will, the criticalness, the severity. How as a child I had the obscure terror that this man could never be satisfied… the man I have sought throughout the world… who branded my childhood and haunted me, I have loved fragments of him in other men."

She continued to look for remnants of her father in her relationships with men—first with Hugh Guiler, an American banker and artist, whom she married at age twenty. He blindly adored her, lavished her with the attention she craved, and supported her artistic life. Shortly after their marriage, they settled in Paris. In August 1925, they moved into their first home in a new building at 11 bis, rue Schoëler. (Notably, this same apartment would later become home to the celebrated feminist writer Simone de Beauvoir, who is also profiled in this book.)

When one understands that the two ongoing themes in Anaïs's life were passion and self-reflection, the steady flow of disparate identities and activities actually make sense. While in Paris, she trained as a flamenco dancer, studied the works of the human psychology pioneers Sigmund Freud, Alfred Adler, and Carl Jung, and underwent analysis herself. Psychology was a relatively new science then, and Anaïs was deeply drawn to it. She was especially interested in the study of how artists make use of real life. Otto Rank's book *Art and Artist* and Jung's approach to the dream realm—"Proceed from the dream outward"—were two important inspirations for how she lived her life. She became a patient of René Allendy, one of the most prominent of the first generation of psychoanalysts, and studied psychoanalysis under Rank, one of Freud's closest disciples. When she later moved to New York, Rank helped her set up a practice as a lay analyst. Both Allendy and Rank eventually fell victim to her seductive charms.

As Bair points out, Anaïs instinctively positioned herself directly in the path of all that was new, avant-garde, and often controversial. She had a knack for recognizing the zeitgeist well before the general public. The list of important literary and artistic talents and thinkers that were a part of Anaïs's life was extensive. It included James Joyce, Marcel Duchamp, Constantin Brancusi, Edmund Wilson, several Beat poets, and Gore Vidal, among others.

> I only believe in fire. Life. Fire. Being myself on fire, I set others on fire. Never death. Fire and life. Les Jeux.

Although she had little formal education, Anaïs's critical writings were well received. Her evaluation of D. H. Lawrence's work drew particular attention. When Lawrence passed away, in 1930, some critics were hesitant to support his writing. But Anaïs recognized that Lawrence had developed a writing style that was in keeping with modern social mores. "Writing about sex directly and with clarity was necessary in [the] modern age," she wrote in 1932's *D. H. Lawrence: An Unprofessional Study*. Soon after, she became one of the first women to explore the realm of erotic writing. To this day, many critics hail her as one of the finest writers of the genre.

Her stories epitomize the language of women's sensuality, so markedly different from that of men. Anaïs's first bestseller was *Delta of Venus*. She called it her literary aphrodisiac, and she described herself in it as "madam of this snobbish literary house of prostitution from which vulgarity was excluded."

As her fame grew, so did her contacts with the famous. Anaïs was an early champion of Henry Miller's, predicting that he would become "the great modernist writer." Theirs was both a working relationship and a love affair. "He is a man who makes life drunk… He is like me," she confided in her diary. Miller too had a lust for life and an appreciation for Lawrence's work. During the years they both lived in Paris, she read and critiqued Miller's work, provided outlines of what he wrote, and supported him financially. Miller, in turn, respected her talent, encouraged her literary endeavors, and even incorporated her ideas and writing into his book *Tropic of Capricorn*.

Anaïs authored many other books, all mined from her varied experiences. *House of Incest*, *Delta of Venus*, and *Little Birds* depict the inner reality of a woman's life. *A Spy in the House of Love* alludes to her own experiences—her female protagonist struggles to forge an intellectual identity and satisfying relationships in the larger world. Bair cites this book as one of the first novels to explore this theme—one that serious novelists have grappled with for the last half century.

After the first volume of Anaïs's diaries was published in 1966, the critic Jean Garrigue's review appeared on the front page of *The New York Times*. It described her writings as "rich and fascinating work… where the volatile human essence has been caught." The literary world had officially taken notice, and Anaïs soon received a deluge of fan mail. She toured the U.S. giving well-attended talks at lecture halls and universities. A lifetime of commendations followed, including honorary doctorates from multiple universities. The United Nations honored her in The Year of the Woman, and the *Los Angeles Times* named her Woman of the Year in 1976.

But controversy also surrounded her. At forty-four, when Anaïs was living in New York with Hugh Guiler, she fell in love with the dashingly handsome young actor Rupert Pole. He lived in California, and was sixteen years her junior. A passionate affair ensued. Anaïs ultimately married him and began a bicoastal double life. For years, she was married to two men at the same time without either's knowledge.

By many standards, she led a morally dubious life. Some critics and literary historians suggest that she didn't always tell the truth in her journals. Either or both may be true, but I suggest an alternate interpretation: Perhaps her diaries are examples of a great experiment, a life lived aspiring to a dreamlike quality. Her life story calls to mind the mythological Greek goddesses: Aphrodite, the goddess of love and sensuality, and Persephone, the goddess of renewal and transformation. Greek gods and goddess were not put on pedestals; they too were depicted with flaws. Mythologies are valued because they reflect the basic patterns of humanity. Anaïs's life and diaries are precisely such—the mythological voyage of a woman toward the pulsating center of her desires. Truth may not be the only prism through which to view the diaries; they are works of art radiating emotional intensity. Others may argue that her many incarnations gave form to her own kaleidoscopic truth, and that truth shifted because she was a different person at different times. As she wrote, "The personal life, deeply lived, always expands into truths beyond itself."

In the last two years of her life, from 1974 to 1976, Anaïs's journals chronicle the pain from the cancer that ravaged her body as well as the constant loving care that Pole showed her in their marriage. In 1976, Anaïs finally revealed her double life to both husbands and asked for absolution. In one of her last letters to Guiler, she wrote, "I am proud to have loved you all my life." Guiler cherished the letter for the rest of his days. Pole, her literary executor, in turn dedicated much of his time and attention to the loving preservation of his wife's memory and the safeguarding and promotion of her work.

As Joseph Campbell wrote in *The Power of Myth:* "All the gods, all the heavens, all the worlds, are within us… People say that what we're all seeking is a meaning for life. I don't think that's what we're really seeking. I think that what we're seeking is an experience of being alive."

Anaïs's life represents a part of us that seeks this kind of vibrancy and passion. "I only believe in fire. Life. Fire," she wrote. "Being myself on fire, I set others on fire. Never death. Fire and life. Les Jeux."

Estée
LAUDER

(1906–2004)

The Alchemist Entrepreneur

For my thirteenth birthday, I received a small but special gift. It was from my glamorous sister-in-law, the stylish one who had lived in Europe, spoke six languages, and carried herself with perfect grace.

"I picked this out myself just for you," she said, handing me a dainty box with a sweet little ribbon. Inside was an Estée Lauder compact of three shimmering shades of eye shadow and a matching tube of lip gloss. It was my first gift of makeup, and it symbolized something bigger in my life: I was on the cusp of becoming a woman and just starting to think about my femininity. Makeup had a special allure—applying a dab of eye shadow or using that lip gloss wand marked a coming-of-age for budding young girls like me.

Since ancient times, women have had a relationship with personal beauty. There is no doubt that grace, confidence, and kindness bring out the inner dimensions of a woman's beauty. But all over the world, women have unique ways of enhancing their physical appearance as well. Accentuating a nice feature, enhancing the radiance of the skin, or dabbing on a scent to create an aura of freshness or sophistication is part of the global ritual of rendering beauty and making the most of what we have been given.

Estée Lauder, businesswoman extraordinaire, understood this better than most. Her advice to people was: "Do you want to succeed? Make the most of what you have."

Indeed, she made the best of her own talents. Her entrepreneurial spirit, her love of beauty, and her keen sense of marketing carried her from the humble streets of Corona, in Queens, New York, to the castles of Europe, building a nearly $8 billion cosmetic empire in more than one hundred fifty countries and territories that today, decades later, remains iconic. And this executive and entrepreneur achieved all these successes without sacrificing her femininity. In fact, she used it to her advantage.

"It seemed obvious from the start that I should use my woman-ness as an asset rather than a liability," she once said. "The art of inventing beauty transcends class, intellect, age, profession, geography—virtually every cultural and economic barrier."

No location was too remote for a personal appearance, no woman too insignificant for a free sample or a skin-care or makeup demonstration. Yet in her heyday she was also lunching with movie stars such as Joan Crawford and having dinner with Princess Grace of Monaco and the Duchess of Windsor. Estée was a woman who created magic for women, making them literally *feel* more beautiful. Her creams added a sense of color to the skin, but they also added glow, radiance, and inner confidence.

When I asked Aerin Lauder to describe her grandmother's role in the cosmetics industry, she agreed that Estée had helped revolutionize the American perfume market. The scents she created—including Youth-Dew, White Linen, and Beautiful—were extracted from flowers,

Previous pages: Portrait of Estée Lauder. ***Above:*** Lauder mixes fragrance, 1981. ***Page 115:*** Lauder and Paulina Porizkova at the launch of the Knowing fragrance at Lord & Taylor in New York City.

What others call tough, I call persistent. It's that
certain little spirit that compels you to stick
it out just when you are at your most tired.

herbs, and essences and reflected the image of the modern woman: classic, independent, and elegant. "Her choice of models [for advertising] was extraordinary, from the elegance of Karen Graham, to the sophistication of Willow Bay, to the European flawlessness of Paulina Porizkova. The models were a reflection of Estée and the brand she built," says Aerin, who now serves as the style and image director for the Estée Lauder brand.

It wasn't always that way, of course. In fact, Estée got her start in business working in a hardware store owned by her father and mother, who were immigrants from the former Czechoslovakia and Hungary, respectively. An uncle, a chemist and skin specialist who created face creams in a makeshift laboratory behind their home, offered her first real experience in cosmetics, sparking a lifelong passion.

Her own first batch of cosmetics was made on the office stove-top with her partner and husband, Joseph. Part chemist, part magician, she transformed her potions into beautifying gold reminiscent of the magical elixirs of medieval alchemists. "We cooked our creams, mixed them, sterilized our pretty new jars with boiling water, poured and filled and planned and packaged," she wrote in her eponymous 1985 autobiography, *Estée: A Success Story*.

Estée was a hands-on businesswoman, and from the start she had a marked gift for promotion. When she opened a small concession booth at the House of Ashe Blondes salon in New York, she put into motion two strategies that are now staples of her industry: First, she was one of the earliest in her field to offer free samples of her products. Advertising by word of mouth would remain a key philosophy of the Estée Lauder brand. Second, Estée pioneered the concept of free demonstrations in which makeup was actually applied in person at the store. She called it "touching faces."

"Most good ideas sparkle in simplicity," she said, "so much so that everyone wonders why no one ever did it before." Her later innovations included mass postcard mailings to women to alert them to special offers, which often included a free gift. This, of course, was the beginning of direct mail marketing, which would soon become the norm in American business.

> People do make their luck by daring
> to follow their instincts, taking risks,
> and embracing every possibility.

Her imprint could be seen in every aspect of the business. "From the beginning, Estée translated her love and passion for style into the brand's advertising, packaging, and store design," recounts Aerin Lauder. The boss herself trained salespeople at Estée Lauder. She was present at the opening of every new store. In the early years, she would even set up her own merchandise. On promotional tours, she made certain to meet with influential editors and fashion writers.

Estée Lauder was no ordinary saleswoman. She knew how important it was to showcase her products at luxury department stores in Manhattan. This was no easy task, as counter space was always at a premium. When she was finally granted a small space at Saks Fifth Avenue, she noted that it was only after her "millionth" request.

"What others call tough, I call persistent," she said. "It's that certain little spirit that compels you to stick it out just when you are at your most tired." Estée's determination was evident from the tiniest details to the most important business negotiations. In order to break into the finest stores, she made personal contacts and was not discouraged by the first or second no. She sometimes waited weeks, months, or, as in the case of Harrods in London, years to convince others that her products were worthwhile.

One day in Houston, Texas, minutes before the Sakowitz department store was about to close, she spotted a woman passing by her counter. It didn't matter to Estée that it was closing time or that she had already slipped off her shoes. She snatched them up and dashed to catch up with "her new convert" just as the unsuspecting woman was about to leave the store. Estée managed to sell her a cream—in less than five minutes. Each customer was important to her, and she grew her business patiently—one woman at a time, one store at time.

Estée was in business at a time when there were few female role models, and juggling her career and personal life was a challenge. Early on, she divorced her husband, Joe, only to realize three years later that he was meant to be her lifelong mate. With their second marriage, they forged a lasting partnership in business as well. Joe managed the production and financial aspects of their enterprise, and the nature of his job allowed him to stay near their home base. Estée, on the other hand, took charge of sales and marketing, which required her to travel often. It worked. For traditional America of the 1940s and '50s, it was a unique and modern relationship.

Theirs was a family business in every sense of the word. Estée and Joe's two sons, Leonard and Ronald, along with their respective wives, were brought into the family firm and had a strong hand in its success and growth. Leonard, who later became CEO, understood the power of globalization early on and paved the way to making Estée Lauder an international brand. He also established the company as a leader in hypoallergenic cosmetics. This, of course, had great appeal for those with sensitive skin, and it led to the creation of the highly successful Clinique label. (At the time, no other fashion-conscious brand had ventured into this much-needed niche.) Within two years of Clinique's launch, no fewer than one hundred eighty companies entered this market. Leonard's wife, Evelyn, became the company's first public relations director as well as the director of new products and packaging. Today, Evelyn is the senior corporate vice president of the Estée Lauder Companies, where she is head of fragrance development worldwide, and the founder and chairman of the Breast Cancer Research Foundation.

Although civic service is Ronald's primary passion, he introduced another line of cosmetics, Prescriptives, and became chairman of Clinique Laboratories, LLC. Jo Carole, Ronald's wife, devised innovative ways to display products using limited counter space.

Estée never wanted to be perceived as masculine in order to compete in the business world. In fact, she embraced her femininity and saw it as a potential business advantage. For instance, she devised her own way of conducting business lunches. She invited colleagues to eat in her office, which was warm and inviting, decorated with soft hues and other feminine touches—the opposite of the typically austere corporate office. She often led them out onto her terrace, which featured a wrought-iron table surrounded by six chairs. "I offered wine. Instead of restaurant silver, I served my own precious sterling, my fine dishes," she said. And she insisted on making a personal connection with her buyers and customers before conducting business.

"Keep away from people who try to belittle your ambitions. Small people always do that, but the really great make you feel that you, too, can become great," Mark Twain once said. Estée embodied that philosophy in her daily life. She surrounded herself with inspiring and supportive people; she wholeheartedly loved her work; she visualized her success and took risks; she dared to act on her dreams; and she avoided distractions. Throughout her career, Estée's mantra was "Be large enough to admit any possibility… make the most of what you have."

Business is not something to be lightly tried on. It's not a distraction, not an affair, not a momentary fling. Business marries you. You sleep with it, eat with it, think about it much of your time. It is, in a very real sense, an act of love. If it isn't an act of love, it's merely work, not business.

An inspiring businesswoman and personality, Estée was repeatedly honored for both her professional accomplishments and her philanthropic efforts, earning, among other distinctions, the French government's insignia of chevalier of the National Order of the Legion of Honor; a place as the only woman on *Time* magazine's 1998 list of the top twenty most influential business geniuses of the twentieth century; and the Spirit of Achievement Award from the Albert Einstein College of Medicine of Yeshiva University.

Today, the Estée Lauder brand remains one of the premier beauty companies in the world, synonymous with luxury, quality, and innovation. And though its founder died in 2004, at the age of ninety-seven, succeeding generations still clearly carry on her spirit. Estée's son Leonard now serves as chairman emeritus of the Estée Lauder Companies and is the senior member of its board of directors. In a 2010 interview in *Women's Wear Daily*, he remarked, "The best teacher I ever had was my mother."

Some say that Aerin Lauder represents the modern version of her legendary grandmother. She too regards her famous forebear as a true role model. "My grandmother taught me the importance of hard work. Her passion and devotion to beauty, and the spirit of the amazing, successful, and long-lasting brand she created influence me greatly." True to Estée's spirit, Aerin launched an eponymous luxury lifestyle brand in April 2011 that will feature her own cosmetics, accessories, jewelry, eyewear, and home products.

And so the magic—and passion—lives on; Estée would undoubtedly be quite pleased.

" A person's power
is as strong as
his or her wish. **"**

Dharma Master Cheng Yen

" It wasn't youth that made me so energetic; it was
enthusiasm. That's why I know a woman of any age
has it within her to begin a business or life's work
of any sort. It's a fresh outlook that makes youth so
attractive anyway, that quality of 'anything's possible.' **"**

Estée Lauder

" Don't give up trying to do what
you really want to do. Where there
is love and inspiration, I don't think
you can go wrong. **"**

Ella Fitzgerald

" Failing is not a crime. What is important
is that if you fail you have the energy and the will
to pull yourself up and keep going. **"**

Wangari Maathai

66 They say I am a fighter. I agree, but I think that, in myself, the fight comes after the dream. 99

Marina Silva

66 Life shrinks or expands in proportion to one's courage. 99

Anaïs Nin

66 In order to be truly creative, you must have the attitude of a beginner. To be a beginner means to maintain innocence and receptivity, for it is only in this way that we can truly and quickly develop our knowledge. 99

Amma

66 You'll never find a better sparring partner than adversity. 99

Golda Meir

Marina SILVA

(1958–)

Environmental and Political Activist, "The Amazon Legend"

It was a typical humid, sunny day in Manaus, a stunning northwestern Brazilian city in the heart of the Amazon rain forest. Music blasted from a nearby kiosk and kids played soccer in the middle of the street underneath a clear blue sky. My family and I followed our guide to a motorboat awaiting us by the shore. We were off to see the "meeting of the waters," a spectacular natural phenomenon where the white water from the Rio Solimões and the dark water from the Rio Negro merge off the coast of Manaus. The light and dark water move downstream for more than five miles without mixing. The Amazon River is formed at the point where the two come together.

The guide explained that the world's largest river was named Amazon by early European settlers: "In Greek mythology, Amazons were brave women warriors who removed one breast so that they could better position a bow and arrow. When the European settlers saw the long hair and body paint of the indigenous people in the area, they actually thought they were women warriors. They thought they were the Amazons," he chuckled, "and that is how this place got its name."

Today, Brazil's warrior woman has a new face: that of Marina Silva. Born into poverty and illiterate until the age of sixteen, but driven by passion, this unexpected paladin of the poor and the environment found her way from the rain forest to a university, then to the political world, and, ultimately, onto the world stage. She is today the region's own living, breathing legend.

Born in 1958 during Amazonia's rainy season, Marina grew up as one of eleven children in Seringal Bagaço, an impoverished community of rubber tappers about forty-five miles east of Rio Branco, the capital of the western state of Acre. The state is in Amazonia, the largest remaining rain forest on earth. Marina and her family lived in a palm-log-and-leaf house on stilts. Her parents were Portuguese and Afro-Brazilian—their ancestors were European colonists and African slaves.

They earned their livelihood from the rubber trees, and their life was simple: They lived without electricity, television, newspapers, or flush toilets. At times, they suffered days without food.

Rio Branco was the closest town with medical care, but the rain forest lacked roads and there were no automobiles in which to drive there. When Marina's mother gave birth to her eleven children, she did so without a doctor and did not go to a hospital. Marina's first brother died from an umbilical cord infection just one week after he was born.

For many years, the family had no sons to perform the hard physical work of clearing forest patches for gardens and tapping rubber trees. Eventually, Pedro, Marina's father, moved the family to Manaus and set up a small store and bar. The business went bankrupt within five months, and after a short time in the town of Santa Maria, near the mouth of the Amazon, back they went to the forest. Pedro then looked to his eldest daughter, Marina, for help.

By the time she was twelve, Marina would wake at dawn and set off to begin walking a ten-mile trail before the sun was up. She would carefully cut into the bark of the rubber trees with her knife and prop a tin cup to catch the white latex sap oozing from the incisions. She would tap nearly one hundred trees before returning home at dusk. By age fourteen, Marina already knew a great deal about the rain forest, yet she could neither read nor write. And she knew practically nothing about the world beyond Seringal Bagaço. In *Marina Silva: Defending Rainforest Communities in Brazil*, a 2001 biography, Ziporah Hildebrandt sums up two important lessons that Marina learned from the rain forest, which became the backbone of her life philosophy in the larger world: "Take only what you need, so that others may live and life continue," and "True love for humanity must be accompanied by a reverence for nature."

Brazil in the mid-1960s was a country in the midst of great change. Amazonia's vast forests were considered empty space, prime for development. In 1970, the government had begun building highways into Amazonia, and new laws gave ranchers subsidies as encouragement to turn thousands of miles of rain forest into pastureland. Millions of poor families were forced from their land to make way for iron and gold mines and giant farms producing food to be sold in Europe and North America. As many as seven thousand families a week flocked to Amazonia to find work. By 1973, when Marina was fifteen, Seringal Bagaço had been divided up into a patchwork of unrecognizable settlement plots. Soon, every year an area of rain forest larger than the state of Massachusetts was cleared and burned. Countless animal and plant species, the known along with the as yet undiscovered, were destroyed.

The bulldozers that cut down the trees left pools and puddles behind, which became a breeding ground for diseases. Two of Marina's younger sisters died from malaria. Then meningitis took Marina's mother's life. Young Marina herself contracted malaria five times but recovered and took on the responsibility of caring for her seven surviving siblings, along with the house. As if these misfortunes were not enough for the Silva family, Marina then contracted hepatitis (most likely attributable to polluted water and malaria medication poisoning) at age sixteen.

Ironically, what seemed like tragedy at the time ultimately helped Marina realize her dreams. She left the rain forest and moved to Rio Branco to get medical treatment, and while there she enrolled in a Catholic school that offered adult literacy classes. She worked full-time as a maid, and in three years completed and passed all the necessary tests to enroll in a university.

I've always had the feeling I would never convince anybody just by my speeches. I had to be a dreamer thinking I could get this far.

While living in the city, she was shocked to see the lowly conditions that thousands of families were subjected to, especially in stark contrast to the dignity with which the poor had lived back home in the rain forest. There was no work and most endured terrible poverty in favelas. This revelation planted the seed in her mind to become involved in working for change. Marina resolved to join the growing social movement of *empates* ("standoffs" in Portuguese) started by political and environmental activists. The *empates* she became involved with were organized by Chico Mendes, a well-known union activist, who was to become Marina's greatest mentor. In 1984, Marina helped to establish Acre's first workers' union.

As the union president, Mendes helped found the Partido dos Trabalhadores (Workers Party). Marina and Mendes both ran for office on the PT ticket—Marina for federal representative, and Mendes for state representative. While neither won, the PT's efforts put environmentalism on the political map.

As Hildebrandt observes in *Marina Silva*, "Just as many trees make a forest, many people make a movement." Together, Marina, Mendes, and other young advocates also arranged nonviolent protest standoffs—often linking arms around giant trees—to prevent the clearing of *seringueiros'* (rubber tappers') land. These human-barrier campaigns against tree felling saved thousands of acres and garnered much attention. However, ranchers and loggers would often beat, kick, and even shoot and kill demonstrators. In 1988, the environmentalists' impassioned leader, Chico Mendes, was assassinated by two ranchers—a great personal tragedy for Marina.

That same year, Marina decided to run for the Rio Branco city council. In her fiery speeches she explained how the plight of the *seringueiros* was directly linked to government policies, and she made vital environmental statistics digestible for the public. For example, Hildebrant notes that "she quoted from studies that proved collecting rubber and Brazil nuts made twenty times more money from the same amount of Amazon land than either farms or ranchers." And she demanded a change in government policies regarding the rights of *favelados*. Marina's energizing vision and voice were contagious and inspiring—more people voted for her than any other candidate in any Acre campaign.

Once in office, she was shocked by her huge paycheck. She promptly went to television stations and newspapers to publicize the large salaries and bonuses that politicians quietly accepted. She filed a lawsuit forcing them to return some of the money they had collected in salaries.

Two years later, in 1990, Marina was elected representative to Acre's state congress. Here, she worked with an environmental organization on a campaign to change World Trade Organization policies. Marina was rapidly becoming the most popular politician Acre had ever seen.

In 1994, at the age of thirty-six, she became the first rubber tapper and the youngest person ever to be elected to Brazil's senate. As a senator, Marina drafted forward-thinking laws controlling Brazil's bioresources: She argued that green technology and a low-carbon economy offer a more promising future than the country's previous reliance on commodities and heavy industry. She supported new farming methods to replace environmentally damaging ones. She was also the leading sponsor of the Environmental Crimes Act of 1998, which made deforestation and illegal logging punishable for the very first time.

Throughout her career, Marina has continued to pursue her own education, working her way toward a postgraduate degree. She has done all this while also raising a family. (Currently Marina has four children—two from her first husband, and two with her present husband.) And her political passions have reflected these values as well: She consistently speaks out for women and children and has written a book about education.

Many awards followed in the wake of her service to the country. In 1996 she was awarded the respected Goldman Environmental Prize, and in 1997 Marina was among twenty-five women designated by the United Nations Environment Program as recipients of an award in honor of International Women's Day. She also won the Champions of the Earth prize in 2007 from the U.N. Environment Program, joining the likes of former U.S. vice president Al Gore and other noted environmentalists.

In 2002, when her fellow Workers' Party founding member Luiz Inácio Lula da Silva was elected president of Brazil, he appointed Marina as his environmental minister. She served in this post for five years, but her tenure was fraught with controversy and criticism. She opposed many projects that she believed would negatively impact the environment, most notably the building of hydroelectric dams and land clearing for biofuel production in the Amazon. During her time in office, the government placed fifty-nine million acres of land under protection, and the country's annual tally of cut forests was chopped in half. After a number of public disputes, she resigned and returned to the senate in 2008.

Page 118: Marina Silva attends a Green Party meeting in Vila Madalena, São Paulo, 2011. *From left:* Silva pauses for a picture with a supporter in Guarulhos, 2010; Silva at the launch of her presidential campaign in Nova Iguacu, May 2010; Environment Minister Silva with Brazilian President Luiz Inácio Lula da Silva in Brasilia, 2004.

Marina would never stop dreaming, "not even for my kids, or my father, or for a man that I love. Exactly because of that my father, my kids, and this man love me."

Then, in May 2010, Marina embarked upon her most impressive historic undertaking to date: The once-illiterate black woman from humble beginnings announced her candidacy for the presidency of Brazil as a member of the Partido Verde (Green Party). That year, at the age of fifty-two, she ran as the first black woman candidate for the presidency of Brazil. Marina's campaign exceeded all expectations by amassing an astonishing twenty million votes (19 percent of the vote). This stunning first-round showing left the other two presidential candidates, Dilma Rousseff and José Serra, without the majority 50 percent of votes to win. Some analysts believe that Marina and her party remained neutral during the final runoff in order to position themselves to run again. Who knows? Perhaps one day Marina Silva may become president of the largest democracy in Latin America.

Driven by her passion for Brazil's land and its people, she has overcome extreme poverty and illness to become the face of the "New Brazil." "They say I am a fighter," Marina told *New Internationalist* magazine in October 1995. "I agree, but I think that, in myself, the fight comes after the dream." She is, without doubt, the Amazon's modern woman warrior.

Gertrude
BERG

(1899–1966)

The First Lady of Television

Weekend afternoons are often lazy times around our house when we relax on the sofa with good books or a movie. So when Netflix delivered a recommended but not so well known 2009 documentary, *Yoo-Hoo, Mrs. Goldberg*, it seemed like a good fit for a Sunday. But in truth I had no idea of the dynamo I was about to discover.

There on my television screen stood a magnetically brash, immensely likable, buxom, apron-clad character. During the late 1940s and early '50s, Gertrude Berg reigned as the First Lady of Television, and she typified the immigrant Jewish mother stereotype of the time. But this was no ordinary Bubbie. She was a brilliant and shrewd businesswoman who wrote thousands of scripts, created a media empire, and launched the first successful television sitcom in America—all long before the famous Lucille Ball.

Polls from the mid-1930s labeled her the second most beloved woman in America—after First Lady Eleanor Roosevelt. And while her career ultimately collided with the dark McCarthy era, her role as a lovable female icon helped ease the nation through the economic woes of the Depression years and alter expectations of women's professional potential.

"I did not get the United States out of the Depression," President Franklin D. Roosevelt once said. "Gertrude Berg did."

She was born Gertrude "Tillie" Edelstein on October 3, 1899, in New York City. She grew up in her home in East Harlem and her family's Fleischmann Mansion Hotel in the Catskill Mountains village of Fleischmanns, New York. Her father, Jake, always wanted his daughter to raise a family and join him in managing the hotel.

But Tillie's paternal grandfather, Mordecai Edelstein, encouraged her to dream. As Glenn D. Smith, Jr., relates in *Something on My Own: Gertrude Berg and American Broadcasting, 1929–1956*,

Tillie's grandfather often reminded her, "It's your America." One afternoon, while strolling together past a New York City theater marquee, young Tillie offered a bold prediction: "See that, Grandpa?" she said, pointing to the name in lights. "My name is going to be there someday."

Tillie's—or rather, Gertrude's—entertainment career was launched in her family's hotel, where she made up clever skits to amuse the visiting children. She also read palms as an amateur fortune-teller.

In her early childhood, Gertrude and her mother, Dinah, were very close. But the untimely death of Gertrude's older brother, Charles, from diphtheria, rocked the household and sent Gertrude's mother into a deep depression that led to several nervous breakdowns.

Gertrude's unstable family relationships left a mark. In later years, the warm, fictional family she created on television may have represented the one she wished for in her own life. As Smith relates: "I think we all live in worlds that are part real, part unreal," she once wrote, "sometimes wishing the real might be touched with just a little of the unreal."

She ultimately found a sense of stability with dashing English chemical engineer Lewis Berg. The two first met in 1914, when he was a guest at her family's hotel. At the time, Gertrude was only fourteen. When Lewis returned several years later to see her again, he was, according to Smith, less than pleased with what he found. In an interview published after her death, Lewis recalls telling her, he "came back to see what kind of person you grew up to be, and I'm disappointed... You've done nothing with your mind, and it's a good mind." He went on, "Give me a little time, and I'll help you to be the kind of woman you want to be." These words both infuriated and excited the ambitious seventeen-year-old. At eighteen, Gertrude married Lewis Berg.

Gertrude had a natural gift for writing, and combined her childhood fantasies with a good deal of creativity and old-fashioned hard work. She spent hours working on stories and refining the skits she had created for earlier performances at the family's hotel. Radio was all the rage in the 1920s, and radio programming often featured real-life family theater. She got her break in 1929—a month after the cataclysmic stock market crash. Gertrude pitched her semiautobiographical, fifteen-minute vignettes, *The Rise of the Goldbergs,* to executives at the National Broadcasting Company on Fifth Avenue in New York. Impressed with her talent, NBC offered her a four-week contract at seventy-five dollars a week. Thus, she became the first woman to write, produce, direct, and star in her own radio series.

The show, the story of an immigrant Jewish family in the Bronx, debuted in November 1929. During that period in American history, Jews were often portrayed as criminals and unsavory characters. The Goldbergs revealed them to be just the opposite. At a time when most lower- and middle-class Americans struggled to put food on the table, the program demonstrated that the

Jewish community suffered the same. Molly, the warm and loving matriarch of the family, offered hope for the American Dream and dispensed homespun wisdom to millions of listeners.

The program was a hit. Three weeks into her first season, Gertrude suffered a sore throat and couldn't go on the air. More than 100,000 people wrote to complain to NBC. Less than two years later, her salary had risen to a then astronomical $2,000 a week, and in eight years to $7,500 a week. In 1931, the show began to air five days a week and became known simply as *The Goldbergs*.

"See that, Grandpa?" young Gertrude said, pointing to someone else's name in lights. "My name is going to be there someday."

Long before Oprah Winfrey or Martha Stewart, Gertrude was, notably, the first woman to succeed in both the creative and business ends of the broadcast industry. During the next two decades, as a result of the show's popularity and her own business acumen, she created a national franchise centered on the Goldberg family concept: two record-breaking vaudeville tours (the latter earning $10,000 a week for Gertrude and her cast, the highest salary ever paid for a vaudeville act); a book; a comic strip; a Broadway play, *Me and Molly*; and a line of *schmattes*— Molly Goldberg–labeled housedresses. The public could not get enough of the Goldbergs.

A sort of hysteria grew around the radio show. The public wanted to know what her characters looked like. Thousand of fans wrote to their local newspapers begging editors to publish photographs of the Goldberg family.

Part of the show's success was directly linked to Gertrude's insistence on authenticity. Her characters spoke naturally. When she cooked a meal as part of the story, they actually cooked it in the recording studio, breaking eggs and futzing with dishes. And although her Jewish characteristics were on full display, it soon became clear that these were all-American traits as well. "I didn't set out to make a contribution to interracial understanding," Gertrude explained in her 1961 autobiography, *Molly and Me: The Memoirs of Gertrude Berg*. "I only tried to depict the life of a family in a background that I knew best. The reactions of the people who listened only showed that we all respond to human situations and human emotions—and that dividing people into rigid racial, economic, social, or religious groups is a lot of nonsense."

As U.S. Supreme Court Justice Ruth Bader Ginsburg—a frequent listener in her younger years—says in *Yoo-Hoo, Mrs. Goldberg:* "Everyone listened to the Goldbergs. Molly was the amalgam of all Jewish aunts and grandmothers." In 1940, at the apex of her radio popularity, Gertrude wrote and acted in an original sketch of *The House of Glass,* a second radio show which she had created in 1935 as part of NBC's first official television broadcast. Her superb comic timing—a critical talent in that up-and-coming industry—was on full display.

After that sketch aired, Gertrude's initial efforts to completely transition her show from radio to television failed. But she didn't accept no for an answer. When the infamous William S. Paley, head of the Columbia Broadcasting System, rejected her proposal, she promptly called him back and got an in-person interview.

Paley knew she had talent but worried about anti-Semitic backlash. By 1949, though, Gertrude had sold him. After a twenty-year radio run, during which she had written most of the show's more than five thousand scripts, she switched from NBC to CBS. With the new televised version of *The Goldbergs*, Gertrude wrote, produced, and acted in America's first family situation comedy. *Life*, *Newsweek*, and *The New York Times* hailed the show as a success.

Although it may seem glamorous now, this was not easy work. She woke at 5:30 each morning to write, rehearse, and then shoot the live 9 p.m. shows. She also supervised the show's production, and became the key spokesperson for General Foods' Sanka Coffee, the program's sponsor. As a result, according to General Foods, Sanka Coffee sales rose by some 57 percent among television viewers. By December 1950, nearly half of all television sets in the New York area were tuned in on Monday nights to her show—then regarded as one of the most valuable theatrical ventures in the entertainment business, worth some $3.5 million in advertising revenues. Molly Goldberg's recurring neighborly call, "Yoo-hoo, Mrs. Bloom!" became a national catchphrase.

And while she was the face of Molly on TV, in reality Gertrude lived a very different life. Earning millions from her various enterprises, she could afford the very best: She had a beautiful Park Avenue apartment, wore exquisite clothes, and collected Picassos and Rembrandts. Great distinctions came her way as well. Gertrude won the first Emmy Award for Best Actress in 1951.

But soon thereafter things began to unravel. At the height of the McCarthy era, Philip Loeb, the great character actor who played Molly's husband, Jake, on the TV show, was accused of being a Communist sympathizer and blacklisted. Loeb, an active actors' union organizer, categorically denied the charges and vowed to clear his name in court. As Smith notes, Gertrude was equally furious. She thought accusing someone of Communist leanings without proof was wholly "un-American." Despite demands by both CBS and General Foods to fire Loeb, Gertrude refused.

She was aware that her actions posed a risk to her own career but she pressed on. She met with sponsor and network representatives and threatened to use her influence and go on every platform imaginable to denounce their actions. Her chutzpah was rewarded; General Foods issued a press release stating that they would retain Loeb.

Eventually, however, the show was cancelled because of Loeb's involvement. Gertrude continued to search for a sponsor that would accept Loeb in spite of his alleged affiliations but to no avail. Ultimately, in 1952, she made the difficult decision to move on without Loeb.

Afraid of being associated with a "Communist," employers and friends alike stopped interacting with Loeb. Three years later, he checked into New York's Taft Hotel under the name Fred Lang ("forever peace" in German) and committed suicide by ingesting sleeping pills. Unbeknownst to Loeb, a week earlier, his file had been officially closed due to lack of evidence.

Gertrude's allegiance to Loeb and her protests against the blacklist irrecoverably damaged her career. Her CBS time slot was given to Lucille Ball, who then became the top star of the network with *I Love Lucy*. In time, Gertrude moved her show to other networks, added new characters, and moved the Goldberg family to the suburbs. But the charm and ethnic tone that made *The Goldbergs* so appealing had been lost.

In the last decade of her life, Gertrude performed in summer stock and appeared on Broadway, where she garnered the best reviews of her career. In 1959, she won a Tony Award for Best Actress for her performance as a widowed Jewish mother in *A Majority of One*.

And that seems a fitting title for the First Lady of Television. This happily married mother of two did what no woman before her had: She broke into and reigned over the male-dominated world of broadcasting. For this, she must always be remembered as a prolific creative force. She resolutely put her passion behind her convictions, whether in her work, her friendships, or her political or philanthropic activities. (In addition to her entertainment successes, she raised millions of dollars in war bonds during World War II, helped with Roosevelt's 1944 reelection campaign, and raised much-needed funds for Jewish refugees.)

Gertrude Berg died in 1966, at the age of sixty-six, of heart failure. Appropriately, Lewis Berg told the *New York Sunday News* several years later, "Gertrude died with her boots on because she wanted it that way."

Somaly
MAM

(1970 or 1971–)

A Voice for the Voiceless

How does a woman who was orphaned as a child, had to forage on her own in the woods for food, and was abused and beaten as a sex slave in a brothel, overcome her grim and desperate circumstances? And perhaps even more miraculously, how does she rise up to become a heroine for so many other vulnerable girls in the same position?

Most people do not have the psychological strength to endure such early atrocities, much less the ability and energy to help others. But Somaly Mam has defied common expectations all her life. Somaly, who has been called the Harriet Tubman of Southeast Asia's brothels, has saved more than five thousand girls in Cambodia and another thousand in Laos, Thailand, and Vietnam. She risks her life on a daily basis to defend the rights of young girls locked into sexual slavery.

> What you have learned from experience
> is worth much more than gold. If you have
> a house it may burn down. Any kind of possession
> can be lost, but your experience is yours forever.
> Keep it and find a way to use it.

I first heard her remarkable story at the 2009 Women's Conference, organized by Maria Shriver, in Long Beach, California. This petite, fine-boned woman stood at the podium before ten thousand women—and held them rapt. Her soft, singsongy voice, sweet smile, and exotic beauty seemed to belie her heartrending account of neglect, poverty, and torture. And while she spoke about the most depraved human acts, the larger themes of her speech were those of triumph and healing. "Sometimes you can learn, even from a bad experience. By coping you become stronger," she said in that darkened auditorium. She talked as if she were confiding in each and every one of us; from time to time she would pause, fighting back tears at her own words.

"Love can mend even the deepest unseen wounds. Love can heal, love can console, love can strengthen, and yes, love can make change," she continued. As one who received very little love growing up, she has given an incredible amount back to the world. Perhaps giving what she lacked the most has been healing not only to the girls she rescues from brothels but also to herself. When the lights came up after Somaly's impassioned speech, there wasn't a dry eye in the room. Within a few seconds, ten thousand women stood in unison to thunderously applaud Somaly Mam, a woman with an indomitable spirit who was able to fight her given circumstances, break the silence of shame, and become the voice for so many young women who have been silenced.

Somaly claims that silence is part of the fabric of her native Cambodian culture. Years of devastation and war under Pol Pot's regime and the Vietnamese occupation have taught her people not to trust anyone. "The more you speak, the more you expose yourself to danger," she notes in her 2008 memoir, *The Road of Lost Innocence*. Of course, silence was essential for survival back then. Today, though, it is generally the cause of more suffering. In an extremely patriarchal and rigid society, women have been taught to be docile and obedient, a mere shadow of who they might be. "Ideally in Cambodia a woman walks so quietly you can't hear her footsteps. She smiles without showing her teeth and laughs softly. She never looks directly into the eyes of any man," she wrote in her memoir, and later, "We're taught when we're little to be like the silk-cotton tree: *dam kor*. Deaf and dumb."

But Carol Gilligan, a renowned feminist writer, professor, and psychologist, believes that regaining one's voice is the biggest link to transformation and healing. "Like a woman claiming her body," she wrote in the foreword to Eve Ensler's *I Am an Emotional Creature*, "a girl claiming her emotions breaks a silence and unleashes a vast resource of clean energy, an energy that can inspire all of us to transform and heal the world." Somaly has done just that. Her courageous act of speaking up has unleashed a global movement.

Human trafficking is a staggeringly fast-growing, multibillion-dollar global criminal enterprise. The sex slave trade, specifically—or, as Kofi Annan, then the United Nations secretary general, called it in 2000, "the worldwide plague" of sex trafficking—has become the world's third most profitable criminal industry, behind only narcotics and weapons smuggling. According to Pulitzer Prize–winning journalist Nicholas D. Kristof, "More women and girls are now trafficked into slavery annually than slaves were transported to the New World at the peak of the transatlantic slave trade."

The social scientist Louise Brown, who has also written extensively on this issue, notes that sexual slavery in Asia is worthy of special attention because of the sophisticated nature of the trafficking networks and their connections to organized crime. In a place where the annual income of more than a third of the population is less than $360, a girl in a brothel who earns fifteen dollars for five days' work is indeed a commodity.

A standard sex-trafficking story goes this way: A girl from a marginalized community—from as young as age five through the late teens—is sold like livestock to a brothel by poverty-stricken parents in debt. The girl acts as collateral and repays the loan by working in a brothel affiliated with the moneylenders. Expenses such as food, clothes, and medicine are deducted from her meager earnings, which oftentimes puts the parents into even more debt. She is unable to refuse clients and cannot escape. If she does, the police may chase her down and return her to the brothel.

Somaly Mam's life also fits into this profile. If you ask what her exact name or date of birth is, she does not know—perhaps 1970 or 1971. "I was called many names. I was called Ya and sometimes Non—'Little One,'" she wrote in her memoir. She doesn't know why her parents turned her over to the care of her grandmother and left when she was a child. She is equally perplexed by why her grandmother abandoned her. With no parents or family, she lived in the forest, eating what she could find. During those early years in the forest, she hardly spoke at all.

An elderly man found her and took her to his home in the Thlok Chhrov village. He gave her a different name: Aya. He claimed to be from the same province as Somaly's father, and she thought there was a chance she might be reunited with her family. But she soon found out that she was to be the man's indentured servant. He beat her regularly and "rented" her out to clean other households. When Somaly was eleven, the man, whom she called Grandpa as a sign of deference, sold her virginity to a local Chinese merchant to pay his debt. Later, he sold her to a soldier. Then one day when the soldier was away, Grandpa took her away once again and sold her to a brothel in Phnom Penh.

As Somaly tells it, there was one glimmer of happiness during those years in Thlok Chhrov. A local schoolteacher, Mam Khon, unofficially adopted her into his family and was instrumental in convincing Grandpa to let her take reading and writing classes. In registering her for school, he gave her yet another name: Somaly, which means "lost in the forest." Although Somaly and Mam Khon's family lost touch once she was sent to the Phnom Penh brothel, Somaly made sure to reconnect with them later in life.

When she arrived in Phnom Penh, her life became a waking nightmare. She was held captive in a dingy, dirty brothel with no running water. She was forced to service five to six clients a day and endured rape and torture. When, around the age of sixteen, she tried to escape, a taxi driver summarily returned her to the madam.

By the late 1980s, humanitarian relief workers from all over the world had come to ravaged, war-torn Cambodia. One such worker encountered Somaly on the streets of Phnom Penh and took a liking to her and brought her into his house. Before he left, he gave her some money and introduced her to Guillaume, another trusted friend. Guillaume, who remains one of Somaly's friends to this day, found her work as a housekeeper and enrolled her at the Alliance Française to learn French. This language became a key to her survival, for she soon met a French aid worker, Pierre Legros, and the two married and left Cambodia. In France with Legros, Somaly began to build her sense of self-worth. Working days as a cleaning lady in a hotel and at a restaurant at night in Cannes, she became confident and self-assured.

In 1994, Legros began working with Doctors Without Borders in Cambodia. Somaly went with him and volunteered her time by handing out condoms and bars of soap to the girls in the brothels. She took the infected and sick girls to the clinic, promising their madams that they would be back by evening. The madams were only too happy to get free medical care for their girls. But Somaly had bigger plans on the horizon.

" I don't feel like I can change the world. I don't even try. I only want to change this small life that I see standing in front of me, which is suffering. "

Pages 130–131: Portrait of Mam by Norman Jean Roy. *Clockwise from top left:* Mam and guests look at photos; Mam speaks with young recruits; a portrait of Mam; *from left*, Mam, Lauren Bush, Ashley Bush, and Sharon Bush attend a party for the Somaly Mam Foundation at The Box; after accepting an award, Queen Latifah announces a large donation to activist and fellow award-winner Somaly Mam at the 2006 *Glamour* magazine Women of the Year Awards.

As she recalls in her memoir, "I (once) needed someone to help me… now I needed to be that person for others." She orchestrated the rescue of an enslaved girl by telling her madam that the girl needed to go to the clinic for a follow-up. This was a high-stakes enterprise, as angry pimps hunt down those who help girls escape, and the police often collaborate with the brothels. But now that Somaly had taken this first daring step, she didn't want to stop.

By 1996, Legros, Somaly, and another friend had created Acting for Women in Distressing Situations (AFESIP), a charity to fund the creation of a center to help the enslaved sex workers. At first, donations were hard to come by, and several rescued girls lived with Legros and Somaly in their own home. Soon, though, Save the Children UK lent them the money to build a center. That first location was inaugurated on March 8, 1997—appropriately, annual International Women's Day. It was at this time that Somaly turned to Mam Khon and her adoptive family in Thlok Chhrov for help. She asked her adoptive mother to come work in the shelter; her adoptive sister taught sewing to the girls, with the aim of helping them to develop a job-friendly skill.

In 1998, after the French journalist Claude Sampère filmed an interview with rescued girls at the shelter, Somaly and her program began to gain international recognition. Funds started streaming in from the European Union and UNICEF, along with support from well-wishers. With the additional money, Somaly began building another shelter, ten miles outside of Phnom Penh.

That same year, Somaly was awarded the prestigious Prince of Asturias Award for International Cooperation. (Notably, Rigoberta Menchú Tum, another visionary profiled in this collection, received the same honor that year. She and Somaly met for the first time at the awards ceremony.) It was a surreal experience for Somaly, a woman who spent her youth working in a brothel, to be greeted by His Royal Highness Felipe de Borbón, Prince of Asturias, and Queen Sofia. Somaly's moving speech at the awards ceremony was met by thunderous applause.

Many more honors have since come her way. Somaly has been awarded the World's Children's Prize for the Rights of the Child in 2008—an accolade she is especially proud of, as the award came from the 6.6 million children who voted. In 2009, Somaly received the Vital Voices Global Leadership Award, along with U.S. Secretary of State Hillary Rodham Clinton and other notable women from around the globe. That same year Somaly was chosen as one of *Time* magazine's 100 Most Influential People in the world. Her awards have helped bring the issue of sex trafficking onto a global platform, which in turn has helped Somaly's fund-raising efforts.

With the money that she received with the Prince of Asturias Award, Somaly set out to build another children's shelter—this time in Thlok Chhrov. As of this writing, fifty-five children call the center their home, and each receives reading and writing lessons from Somaly's adoptive father, Mam Khon. The center rescues and raises girls as young as six years old.

Since its inception, AFESIP has brought approximately two thousand cases before the courts; set up training programs to teach cooking, weaving, and hairdressing; and built a network of doctors, psychologists, and social workers to address the girls' various needs. To ease the reintegration of the girls back into society, each is assured a job in a safe environment. Social workers remain in contact with the girls through monthly visits. AFESIP now has offices in Siem Reap, Cambodia; Vietnam; Thailand; and Laos. Its network of support throughout Southeast Asia has become essential, as many girls are sent across borders to work. In 2007 Somaly created the Somaly Mam Foundation with partners in the United States. This organization runs awareness and advocacy campaigns in North America and hopes to involve the public and governments in the fight to abolish modern-day slavery.

> I strongly believe that love is the answer and that it can mend even the deepest unseen wounds. Love can heal, love can console, love can strengthen, and yes, love can make change.

This fight has cost Somaly in some ways. Now a mother of three, she has been personally threatened repeatedly. One of her daughters was even abducted but luckily found. She is no longer married to Legros. Today, although Somaly says that the scars of her old life remain, she feels lucky that she can help society's most vulnerable.

Somaly's life is a testament to several lessons, including: One must never underestimate a person's true potential; giving love can be as healing as receiving it; and one person's dream can indeed make a significant difference in the world.

It was in the spirit of highlighting women's grassroots efforts all over the world that Anne Firth Murray, a Stanford University professor and the founding president of the Global Fund for Women, wrote her book, *From Outrage to Courage*. In its prologue, she quotes the following passage from the Talmud: "Do not be daunted by the enormity of the world's grief. Do justly, now. Love mercy, now. Walk humbly, now. You are not obligated to complete the work, but neither are you free to abandon it."

Somaly's work truly embodies this sentiment. As she wrote in her memoir: "I don't feel like I can change the world… I only want to change this small life that I see standing in front of me… This small real thing that is the destiny of one little girl. And then another, and another…"

Dharma Master CHENG YEN

(1937–)

Spiritual Leader, Founder of Tzu Chi, "Master of Compassion"

One of the most important international charities and religious movements in the world is, surprisingly, one that you've probably never heard of. Incredibly, most of the West has not. But when New York City's World Trade Center was attacked on September 11, 2001, it was the only charity that offered immediate cash relief to victims' families. Similarly, it raised $85 million for disaster relief for tsunami victims in Southeast Asia in 2004 and a total of $514 million for poor communities in more than seventy developing countries. When Hurricane Katrina struck the Gulf Coast of the United States, in August 2005, wreaking havoc on New Orleans and other areas, this group arrived on the scene with $5 million to donate to victims.

So what is it? Driven by a mission of universal compassion, the Taiwan-based Tzu Chi Foundation is ten million members strong, with an endowment closing in on $1 billion. And a single woman animates it all: the organization's founder, Dharma Master Cheng Yen.

She is a penniless Buddhist nun, and her presence is said to permeate every aspect of the Tzu Chi Foundation. A petite, quiet, and truly modest woman, Dharma Master Cheng Yen has inspired millions to volunteer in forty-seven countries around the globe. She has infused the foundation—the largest nongovernmental organization in the Chinese-speaking world—with her motto: "Instruct the rich and serve the poor." Through her efforts, along with those of her volunteers, eleven million victims of wars, floods, and earthquakes around the world have received aid; and schools, scholarships, and outreach clinics have been established in twenty-seven American states. I came across her by chance, only to learn that Tzu Chi even operates in my own backyard, giving free meals to the homeless in Los Angeles.

Open the door to your heart. If you open the door, anyone can go in and out. On the other hand, if the door is too narrow, everyone will bump into it… Life is happiest when you are needed by others and can do things for others… A loving heart is the most beautiful thing in the world.

According to biographer Mark O'Neill's *Tzu Chi: Serving with Compassion*, Dharma Master Cheng Yen says, "The act of giving brings as much blessing to the donor as the recipient." She insists that Tzu Chi members deliver all aid in person. Dressed in blue shirts and white trousers, her volunteers provide food, first aid, and temporary housing whenever disaster strikes. Their support is also often therapeutic: They listen to victims' stories, and believe that healing the soul is just as important as healing the body. Their visits usually feature a smile and a thank-you for allowing them to make a contribution. Indeed, for Tzu Chi members, the act of giving is part of their own spiritual growth.

As O'Neill relates, Dharma Master Cheng Yen says her ultimate goal is "to bring Buddhism back to its original form, as Buddha had wanted it to be twenty-five hundred years ago." Her religious movement is not confined to chanting scriptures in temples and monasteries. Underequipped hospitals and downtrodden, earthquake-damaged neighborhoods have superseded the traditional Buddhist monastery as places to practice *tzu* ("love and kindness") and *chi* ("mercy"). She calls this Humanistic Buddhism or Buddhism in Action. Good Buddhists, she says, must try to bring out the Buddha within themselves. Giving willingly and without regard to race, religious affiliation, or background is the ultimate expression of nonexclusive love.

The Mother Teresa of the Far East, as she is often called, was born in 1937 in Qingshui, a small town in Taichung County, Taiwan. She had just a primary school education. In her youth, the beautiful Chin-yun (Cheng Yen's birth name) attracted plenty of smiles from potential suitors. But she dreamt of a service-filled life: She wanted to be a positive force—not just for her own family but for all of humanity.

Chin-yun decided early on that she needed to move beyond her simple home to achieve her grand goals, so she decided to leave and become a nun. Twice she ran away, but her family discovered her whereabouts and brought her back. However, her resolve was unshakable; at twenty-four she left for good and embarked on her spiritual path.

It did not take long for Chin-yun to realize that she did not fit in at the Buddhist temples she visited. She disagreed philosophically with every "master" she met. For example, she felt that asking Buddha to perform miracles was irrational and that monks and nuns should not accept money for performing religious services.

Previous pages: Tzu Chi Foundation's Dharma Master Cheng Yen at her desk. *Clockwise from top left:* Cheng Yen converses, 1996; a volunteer digs through recycled plastic bottles, used to make blankets, at the Tzu Chi Foundation factory in Taipei, Taiwan; a Filipino fire victim receives a hot meal from a volunteer, 2011.

What she really wanted was to inspire others—and a temple of her own. She went to the Lin Chi Temple in Taipei and asked to be initiated. She was told that this was impossible unless a master sponsored her. And there she met the revered Master Yin Shun.

Some have said this meeting was a striking example of Buddhist providence—a preordained event that was the seminal moment in Chin-yun's life. Master Yin Shun was a respected monk and an internationally acclaimed Buddhist scholar, and had only accepted four disciples in his life prior to Chin-yun. However, when she approached and asked him to sponsor her, he obliged.

As he explained later, a voice inside him said it was his karma to be her master and her karma to be his disciple. He became her closest adviser. He gave her the name Cheng Yen when she was ordained. According to O'Neill, Master Yin Shun told her that her mission was to "serve all living beings and enlighten them with Buddhism."

By 1964, at twenty-seven, Cheng Yen had accepted five female disciples of her own. The six lived together happily in a small hut. But two major incidents prompted her to create Tzu Chi: The first took place when she visited a patient at a local clinic. There she saw a large pool of blood on the ground. The staff explained that a pregnant aboriginal woman—in need of an operation—had made an eight-hour journey over the mountains to the clinic. But when the clinic workers demanded a deposit of $200 for care, the family could not pay. The woman was refused medical help and lost her baby. Cheng Yen promised herself that she would try to build a hospital in which the needy would have access to medical care. As Dharma Master Cheng Yen tells followers, "When a promise is made to your heart, sooner or later your heart will remind you to carry out that promise."

The second incident occurred one Sunday, when three Roman Catholic nuns came to visit her in her hut to discuss religion and philosophy. Before leaving, they asked her why the Buddhist community was not active in the surrounding area. The Catholic Church, they pointed out, served communities by building hospitals, nursing homes, and schools. Why didn't Buddhists?

What counts is not the length of life but how it is lived. If a person performs good deeds and helps others, it is a life full of merit.

It was then that Cheng Yen decided to establish her own charity. In 1966, she set up headquarters in Hualien, a poor town on Taiwan's eastern coast. Despite these humble beginnings, her vision was enormous. As O'Neill notes, Cheng Yen teaches, "We should not underestimate the power of smallness." At first, the odds seemed stacked against her. Here was a relatively uneducated nun with just five disciples, living in a remote corner of Taiwan. She suffered from a heart condition that did not allow her to fly outside her country, yet she dreamt of building hospitals and helping the needy around the world. Her first followers, in addition to her disciples, were thirty housewives. They raised money by weaving woolen sweaters and baby shoes. The housewives each saved two cents a day, and each disciple sewed one extra pair of baby shoes every day to sell. Together, they saved $33 a month. According to O'Neill, Cheng Yen was encouraged, even happy, saying, "The act of giving, however little, is more important than the amount."

From these modest beginnings, the Tzu Chi Foundation slowly evolved into the biggest nongovernmental organization in the Chinese-speaking world, powered primarily by its volunteers' deep trust in and devotion to Dharma Master Cheng Yen and her cause. Tzu Chi's sophisticated operation provides transparent financial reporting as well, in which donors choose specific projects, and accounts are notified of when and how money is being spent. It is now the richest NGO in Taiwan, with annual donations of $300 million and an endowment of $800 million.

Financial gifts come from prominent business leaders, politicians, and celebrities, along with families and individuals at all levels of society. It has the biggest bone marrow bank in Asia and has built seven hospitals, one hundred schools, and a university. Tzu Chi's expansive recycling program includes 200,000 people and forty-five hundred recycling centers, and turns plastic bottles into polyester blankets. Dharma Master Cheng Yen herself was nominated for a Nobel Peace Prize in 1993.

Other factors have also helped. From the start, Cheng Yen made a number of critical decisions that changed the course of her foundation. For example, when she embarked upon building the first hospital in Hualien, she refused a donation of $200 million from a single Japanese developer. People were shocked, but Cheng Yen believed the hospital should be built with gifts from thousands of individuals so that each donor would have a sense of personal ownership in the project. As O'Neill observes, she believes the hospital (along with every other project) presented an opportunity to "awaken the goodwill" of thousands of people who would never have contributed had she accepted the single donor's money.

Several projects are incredible success stories. The Tzu Chi General Hospital is the first Buddhist hospital built in China in two millennia. It is the first hospital in Taiwan where admission is free and the poor receive medical care at no cost. To attract doctors and nurses, it operates its own medical school, a nursing college, and a medical research center. It stands in the poorest area of Taiwan, and aspires to become the Mayo Clinic of the Far East. In the past five years, $10 million has been invested in world-class equipment so doctors can provide better care and attempt pioneering research in their fields. Hospital administrators are expected to take part in volunteer activities. This vision of compassion and care permeates all of Tzu Chi's projects.

Love and mercy transcend races, nationalities, and geographical distance.

So how does a woman with limited education who cannot travel outside of Taiwan lead a global community? In some ways, Tzu Chi runs more like a multinational corporation than a charity. Members are on call twenty-four hours a day. Cheng Yen communicates with constituents via satellite telephone and video chats. She has her own TV station, which broadcasts through twelve satellites, allowing her to reach 80 percent of the world's population. She stays apprised of world events via dozens of television channels; her staff reports on ongoing projects and future plans.

Many followers believe Dharma Master Cheng Yen was born with wisdom gained in previous lives. Others say the depth of her compassion shows in her radiant face, which allows her to affect people deeply with few words. Most importantly, though, she has attracted a large group of followers with the intensity and integrity of her own beliefs. As O'Neill notes, she tells them: "Open the door to your heart. If you open the door, anyone can go in and out. On the other hand, if the door is too narrow, everyone will bump into it… Life is happiest when you are needed by others and can do things for others… A loving heart is the most beautiful thing in the world."

Through her conviction and love, Dharma Master Cheng Yen has embraced the entire world as her family. Her benevolent vision has motivated the goodwill of millions and created a remarkable global movement that not only serves our neediest brothers and sisters but also immeasurably enriches and inspirits the humanity of those who give.

Zaha HADID

(1950–)

Nature's Architect

It was a humid summer day in the Italian countryside. While thousands of art aficionados strolled Venice's serpentine streets, exploring La Biennale's exhibitions, I had decided to tour the famed Palladian villas just outside the city. Built in the sixteenth century by Andrea Palladio—widely regarded as the most influential person in the history of Western architecture—these jaw-dropping Renaissance masterpieces celebrate order and balance; in Palladio's world, simple geometric forms reign.

It is very important to be optimistic,
or it will bring you down.

As I stepped through the entrance of the Villa Foscari La Malcontenta, Palladio's principles of proportion and symmetry were on full display. I happily strolled from one well proportioned room to the next. Then came the surprise of my visit.

Standing almost defiantly in the center of a Giovanni Battista Zelotti–frescoed room was a giant white, asymmetrical, and most curvaceous installation. I recognized it instantly. Zaha Hadid's signature was all over the piece. Famous for her slick, sculptural, often futuristic designs—and for consistently redefining the limits of her medium—the Iraqi-born, London-based Zaha is one of the world's most respected architects.

The juxtaposition of Zaha's powerful, curving form and Palladio's classicism was unexpected—and magnetic. Apparently, the Fondazione La Malcontenta had asked Zaha and her partner to create two installations for the villa in honor of the five-hundredth anniversary of Palladio's birth, in 2008. Side by side, the two designers crossed half a millennium of

architectural discourse. Together, they offered the perfect context for appreciating the latter's work—born of a vision unconstrained by any one time or place.

Zaha has always been ahead of her time. For years she sketched and designed groundbreaking projects, her vision consistently beyond material possibilities. Even today, with the advent of digital technology, the material world is just beginning to catch up to the imaginations of architects like Zaha.

"There are 359 other degrees. Why limit yourself to one?" she has said. With continuously curving walls and layered, flowing spaces, Zaha's avant-garde designs are metaphors for nature: sand dunes, waves, shells, and cocoons. These are buildings that stop you in your tracks; their organic elements are familiar enough to make them accessible, their drama potent enough to make your heart race.

Zaha may be the world's most admired female architect, but she has proven to be a prolific designer as well. She has created a furniture line, reinterpreted the Lacoste shoe and the iconic Louis Vuitton bucket bag, and put her stamp on a hydrogen-powered three-wheel automobile called the Z-Car. When I asked about her interest in other design arenas, she said, "I see it as a part of a continuous process of design investigation… The pieces are experimental, quicker to execute than the architectural projects, and [they] inspire creativity."

But no matter the medium or scale—whether a shoe or an opera house—a sense of movement is inherent in her designs. When you sit on one of her benches, your first reaction is to slide your hands over the smooth surface, connecting with its current. When entering one of her buildings, you may experience an uncanny feeling that space is unraveling before you as one room flows into the next. When the talk show host Charlie Rose asked Zaha to describe the defining characteristic of her work, she responded: "I liberated certain norms in architecture… the designs allowed for possibility."

These days, Zaha is enjoying unprecedented acclaim and has multiple global commissions under way. She is the first woman to have won the Pritzker Architecture Prize, considered the top honor for a living architect. She has been recognized as a Commander of the Order of the British Empire, and was awarded honorary degrees from Yale University and Pratt Institute. In 2008 she was included in *Forbes* magazine's list of the World's 100 Most Powerful Women, and in 2010 she was on *Time* magazine's list of the World's 100 Most Influential People.

However, her road to architecture superstardom was a long and often bumpy one. Architecture is regarded as the most masculine of the arts, and this was especially evident when Zaha began her career, more than thirty years ago—as were misgivings regarding her Iraqi background. When I asked about stereotypes in architecture, she replied that much has changed in favor of women in the past fifteen years. As a female architect, however, "the irony is that I

Previous pages: Portrait of the architect by Steve Double. ***Clockwise from top left:*** Inside the Hadid-designed London Aquatics Centre; Hadid's Guangzhou Opera House; Hadid in her apartment in Clerkenwell, Central London, 2008; Hadid receives the Praemium Imperiale medal in Architecture at a ceremony in Tokyo, Japan, 2009. ***Page 150:*** Hadid's design for the MAXXI museum in Rome.

> **❝** I started out trying to create buildings that would sparkle like isolated jewels; now I want them to connect, to form a new kind of landscape, to flow together with contemporary cities and the lives of their peoples. **❞**

don't really experience [resistance] in the Arab world or the Far East," she says. "It is more obvious in the West, particularly the Anglo-Saxon world."

Born in Baghdad in 1950, Zaha was raised in a well educated Islamic family. Her parents came from distinguished families and her father was the leader of a liberal Iraqi political party. In the 1950s and '60s a spirit of optimism and development swept across what was then a progressive Iraq. The new buildings cropping up all over Baghdad impressed the young Zaha. By the time she was a mere eleven years old, she knew she wanted to be an architect.

One notable family vacation to southern Iraq when she was a teenager made an indelible impression on her aesthetic sense. "My father took us to see the Sumerian cities," she told *The Guardian* in 2006. "The beauty of the landscape—where sand, water, reeds, birds, buildings, and people all somehow flowed together—has never left me." Zaha has often said that she has been trying to discover and invent a form of architecture that translates that early experience in a contemporary way.

Zaha studied mathematics at the American University of Beirut, and her family left Iraq after Saddam Hussein came to power. They relocated to London, where she became a British citizen and enrolled at the Architectural Association School of Architecture.

"She was very noticeable," Dutch architect Rem Koolhaas recalled in 2009, describing his star student in an article about Zaha by John Seabrook in *The New Yorker*. "She was dressed in a way that forced you to notice her, but very stylish." Richard Weinstein, a professor and dean emeritus of UCLA's Graduate School of Architecture and Urban Planning, was left with a similar impression. "Zaha certainly has a commanding presence. She is forthright, strong and direct, exceptionally intelligent, [and] has a wonderful sense of humor with her deadpan remarks. And, of course, she is very fashionable," he told me.

> I liberated certain norms in architecture…
> the designs allowed for possibility.
> Whenever you do something which is
> not normative and part of the status quo,
> which is not corporate, you struggle.

She is known for her capes, Issey Miyake jackets, and gossamer layers. With her Middle Eastern features and flashing, dark eyes, Zaha makes a dramatic impression.

But in graduate school it was her drawings that caused a stir. Her graphic expressions were inspired by Russian avant-garde artists such as Kazimir Malevich, who painted layered geometrical masses, and Wassily Kandinsky, with his flowing lines. Apparently no one understood what she was doing, but Koolhaas was fascinated and encouraged her. Those drawings eventually gave way to Zaha's singular creative voice.

In 1980 Zaha opened her own office. Her designs won competitions, but none of them were built. With a small client base, she was best known as a paper architect. Her renderings for The Peak, a sports club to be erected on the mountain slopes of Hong Kong, won first prize in a design competition, but plans for its construction fell through. It was to be ten long years before she got a major commission: a small fire station on the grounds of the Vitra design and manufacturing complex, in Weil am Rhein, Germany, which has now been converted into a museum. By the time construction was finished on the fire station, things were looking up—and Zaha was positioned for a breakthrough.

In 1994, her design for the new Cardiff Bay Opera House in Wales was selected for construction. But Zaha and her designs were also under sharp attack. England's Prince Charles supported a widely publicized campaign in favor of neo-traditional architecture, while others turned a quizzical eye when they learned that an Arab woman interested in abstraction had created the unusual design.

A Welsh member of Parliament said the opera house's design "was identical to the shrine in Mecca," and warned that the building would become a target for a fatwa, reported Seabrook in *The New Yorker*. Zaha suffered snide remarks about her background and her status as a single woman. The project's backers finally withdrew their commitment. Zaha was devastated.

But she pressed on. The name Hadid means "iron" in Arabic—and iron-willed she is. Zaha refused to compromise her creative ideas, even when few of them were being realized. "In architecture, one has to have a tremendous will [to survive]," she said in a 2010 CNN interview. It's "really a very tough profession."

Her big break finally came eighteen years after she set up her own firm. In 1998 she was commissioned to build the Lois & Richard Rosenthal Center for Contemporary Art, in Cincinnati, Ohio. The facade of the museum was built at various angles, and the galleries inside differed in shape and size, overturning the long-standing idea that museums had to present neutral spaces for art. The museum—the first in the United States designed by a woman—was proclaimed by *The New York Times* to be "the most important American building to be completed since the end of the Cold War." According to *The New Yorker*, Aaron Betsky, the director of the Cincinnati Art Museum, claims her designs offer a different way of seeing: "We don't have to accept reality—she will unfold her own reality."

Other high-profile projects soon began streaming in, and inspiration from nature remained integral to her designs. The Phaeno Science Center, in Wolfsburg, Germany, looks like a three-sided boulder; its interior walls are reminiscent of sand dunes. Italy's National Museum of XXI Century Arts, known as MAXXI, is a three-story structure with no main facade and no delineated front and back. Inside, walls cross and intersect, evoking a feeling of gliding inside a wave. (Notably, early on, Zaha's firm turned to shipbuilders, since they knew how to work with the elastic curves of ships' hulls.)

An oft-cited criticism of her work is that her buildings may overwhelm the viewer. "Would they say that about landscape?" she has asked in her own defense. "Do people get overwhelmed when they go to a mountain or a park?... We try to do something that makes an impression more

like a landscape." Looking at the long list of global commissions that she has earned, it is safe to say that many institutions are vying for this kind of experience.

The Guangzhou Opera House is an eighteen-hundred-seat venue that dominates the riverfront of Guangzhou, China's Zhujiang New Town business district. It has been heralded as one of Zaha's major triumphs. The exterior of the building is said to be a poetic analogy of two rocks in a stream. Fluid lines and cascading staircases abound inside. Guests can peek through triangular windows in the entrance hall to catch a glimpse of the city's skyline.

> Architecture is about well-being, that people
> should feel good whether they are in a hospital,
> an office building, or a plant or a house.

Pushing the boundaries of how architecture is perceived, Zaha gives people new opportunities to experience and interact with their environment. In the past, some clients would take one look at her fantasylike plans and promptly announce that her design could never be built. But Richard Weinstein notes that "her superintelligence makes for a powerful, if not intimidating, presentation of her ideas." Ultimately, many are swayed by her uncommon vision. "I still believe in the impossible," she has said.

Zaha also has a keen business sense. She employs more than three hundred fifty people and has grouped them into teams. Like her architecture, these teams are fluid, with no obvious hierarchy. Often they collaborate based on a project's location. Her current challenge is to oversee all the projects in the pipeline simultaneously. At the time this book goes to press, she has more than fifty under construction—and counting.

In the not-so-far-off future, we all may be able to walk through some of Zaha's newest designs: the Eli and Edythe Broad Art Museum of Michigan State University, in East Lansing, Michigan; a high-speed train station in Naples, Italy; a performing arts center in Abu Dhabi; a museum in Taipei, Taiwan; and the London Aquatics Centre, the architectural showcase of the 2012 Olympics. By far one of the most personal, poignant projects for Zaha is the design of the new headquarters for the Central Bank of Iraq—viewed by many as a symbol of the new nation. "It doesn't matter how long you live outside your country, there is something wonderful about speaking the language and understanding the culture… It will be quite an emotional return when I do go back, as I don't know anyone there anymore." Still, she is thrilled and touched by the opportunity to do something in her native land.

With so many projects under way and several more yet to be realized, Zaha is reinterpreting our world—not just building by building, but whole environments at a time.

Jacqueline NOVOGRATZ

(1952–)

The Conscious Capitalist

As I mulled over the choices for the last visionary woman to include in this collection, I knew I wanted to showcase someone whose work reflects today's globalism, innovation, and commitment to social action. At the same time, I wanted her to be an amalgam of every other woman in this book: curious, fearless, passionate, and committed. But who?

The answer, once before me, was simple: Jacqueline Novogratz, the author of the best-selling book *The Blue Sweater: Bridging the Gap Between Rich and Poor in an Interconnected World*. A former banker who established a women's microfinance bank in Rwanda, and a businesswoman who is changing the face of philanthropy globally, Jacqueline is a woman who follows her passions.

However, the answer did not present itself immediately. I hadn't heard of Novogratz until just months before I began writing this book. Thanks to a little synchronicity, though, one evening I found myself at a friend's dinner party, seated next to a fascinating woman—Judy Olian, the dean of the Anderson School of Management at UCLA's graduate business school. She sang Novogratz's praises. The very next day, my husband randomly e-mailed me about an upcoming Novogratz lecture at Los Angeles's Milken Institute. And that was that.

Two days later, I found myself sitting in a packed auditorium, rapt, as the tall, blond, athletic woman standing before me shared her inspiring life story and her pioneering philanthropic efforts. As a twentysomething, Jacqueline Novogratz walked away from a successful career on Wall Street to work with the poor in Africa, ultimately founding the Acumen Fund in 2001. A cross between venture capitalism and a traditional charity, Acumen's mission is to invest in emerging leaders and breakthrough ideas to help in the fight to end world poverty. It invests globally in daring entrepreneurs who wish to build businesses that offer essential services such as

affordable health care and housing, safe drinking water, and alternative energy for the poorest of the poor. The success of these enterprises is measured in terms of capital flowing back to the fund and, most important, in social impact. In 2010 alone, Acumen's investments reached some forty million people, and Jacqueline has her sights set on reaching millions more.

> I was out to change the world, to know it
> and to love it for all its exquisite beauty
> and perfection as well as for its flaws.

"I went to Africa to try to save the continent," she said, "only to learn that Africans neither wanted nor needed saving." Her experiences there framed her perspective on what real assistance means: providing opportunities so that others may live up to their potential.

As she spoke, Jacqueline exuded a sense of optimism that was nothing less than contagious. Describing poignant meetings with people from a broad range of communities—from villagers in remote Indian outposts to struggling farmers in rural Kenya—she explained how our planet is changing as we redefine the world community. "As global citizens," she said, "we now share more common values that connect us, regardless of gender, class, or ethnicity."

When asked what she thought defined a great leader, Jacqueline replied: "Being a great listener. The entrepreneurs we work with have to listen to the poor to understand who their customers are—how they make decisions, what they prefer when it comes to basic needs. And being a great listener means that if an approach isn't working, you're willing to step back and innovate to try something new."

The sequence of events that led me to Jacqueline reminds me of a famous quote by the Brazilian novelist Paulo Coelho: "When you want something, the whole universe conspires to help you realize your desire." It also appears that serendipitous incidents may have marked Jacqueline's career path—each one helping to lead her to where she is today.

She stumbled upon her first as a young banker working in Rio de Janeiro. There, Jacqueline got a firsthand glimpse of the modern era's economic disparity. She saw big banks writing off millions of dollars of bad debt for wealthy clients while low-income citizens were barely making a living in the nearby favelas, or slums. One story she tells is particularly striking. In Rio, she met a six-year-old named Eduardo who lived on the streets. One day she brought him to her hotel and treated him to a hamburger by the pool. The manager immediately asked her to take him off the premises. During the next few days, Jacqueline thought a lot about this unsettling incident. She also began to consider how the world's banking system might be used to make lasting changes in the lives of marginalized people.

Determined to make a difference, Jacqueline requested a meeting with her boss and suggested that their bank start experimenting with loans to Brazil's working class. Her supervisor rejected her ideas and warned her that she might need to reconsider her future with the company. "You laugh too loudly and dress like Linda Ronstadt," he said. "You are friendly with everyone, and I worry that executives might mistake you for one of the secretaries."

While such comments might have deterred other people, Jacqueline only became more resolute. "I couldn't imagine stifling my laugh in order to succeed," she said. Besides, her dream was to use her financial skills for a higher purpose. She soon began working for a nonprofit microfinance organization for women based in New York City.

Her first stint in this new job took her to Nairobi, the capital of Kenya, where she attended a women's conference. There she met a woman who later invited her to establish a credit system and a financial institution for Rwandan women—a very progressive idea for the East African nation. Until recently, Rwanda had not even allowed women to open bank accounts without the written permission of their husbands.

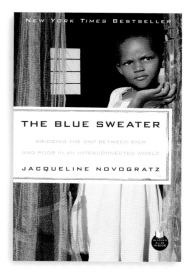

> ❝ How you see where you are always depends on where you've been. ❞

Another chance meeting awaited her in the streets of Kigali, the capital of Rwanda—one that would have a remarkable impact on the rest of her life. One day, she spotted a young boy wearing a familiar but worn blue sweater. She approached him and was utterly amazed to learn that it was the very same sweater she had donated to Goodwill as an eleven-year-old in America—her name was still on the label. Jacqueline was completely taken aback by the sheer improbability of seeing her own sweater make a fourteen-year trek to another continent. This fluke incident cemented her belief that a simple act can reverberate through time and place, truly affecting another person's life. It has become the motivating philosophy of her life's work. (The title of her best-selling book comes from this incident.)

In Rwanda, Jacqueline found herself working sixteen-hour days while learning a new language on the fly. But she was energized by the task at hand. She truly believed that by lending money—instead of giving charitable handouts—to poor women, they could become active participants in building their own lives with a sense of dignity. "Freedom," Jacqueline says, "is not just about political liberty but also about economic independence and the power of choice." With the help of others, she established Duterimbere, a nonprofit microfinance organization that provides credit, loans, and business training for Rwandan women. To date, Duterimbere has served more than fifty thousand clients and helped countless women establish thriving businesses.

When Jacqueline returned to the United States, two mentors helped shape her new vision for social change. While studying for an MBA at Stanford University, she met John William Gardner, who had served as Secretary of Health, Education, and Welfare from 1965 to 1968 under President Lyndon Johnson and went on to found Common Cause in 1970. "Everything John did was about releasing human energies at all levels of society," she said. Gardner placed a premium on people learning from one another across ethnic, religious, and socioeconomic lines and spoke of the importance of fostering a sense of community that transcends geography. Through his lectures and in subsequent conversations, she learned what was to become a cornerstone of her firm's philosophy: that great social movements need both insiders and outsiders to make change happen.

She also relied on the wisdom of Peter Goldmark, Jr., the charismatic president of the Rockefeller Foundation (1988–97), where she served as a fellow. Goldmark, too, stressed the need for creating global bonds, but he also helped Jacqueline study how philanthropy can merge with sound business practices to help solve social problems. These principles are at the heart of the Acumen Fund's strategy today.

When the time came to begin investing in various enterprises, a colleague offered her valuable advice: "Just start. Don't wait for perfection. Just start and let the work teach you," the colleague said. "You'll learn more from your mistakes than you will from your early successes, anyway."

In relatively few years, Acumen has had a tremendous impact on the lives of millions. To date, Acumen's investments have created about forty thousand jobs globally. Since a third of the world's poorest residents live in India, and they have limited access to sanitary, well-equipped health care, this vast country has been a focus point. Acumen has been involved in a joint venture with an Indian-owned company to bring low-cost obstetrics, including prenatal, childbirth, and postnatal care to poor women. Nine LifeSpring hospitals have been established in India, where an estimated seventy thousand expectant mothers can now pay eighty dollars (one-third of the cost of services at a regular hospital) to receive maternity care.

Another remarkable success for the fund has come in the field of energy. It is hard to imagine that as many as 375 million people in rural India lack access to electricity. With the help of Acumen, Gyanesh Pandey, an Indian entrepreneur, has created plants that generate power from abundant agricultural waste matter—rice husks. The electricity is carried to households via insulated wires running along bamboo poles. The first plant was built in 2007; now sixty-five mini power plants exist, changing the way 150,000 people live and work. Within the next five years, the company wants to bring electricity to five million people living outside the current electrical grid.

Today, Acumen's social-impact initiatives are spread across the world, including housing projects and the first commercial mortgages for the poor in Pakistan, access to affordable hybrid seeds for farmers in Kenya, access to clean water through innovative ultraviolet filtration technology in more than 280 villages in India, and the production of long-lasting, insecticide-treated bed nets in the East African country of Tanzania that have improved more than thirty million lives. In addition, each year, ten promising emerging leaders from around the globe are selected for leadership training, along with operational and financial guidance, through the Acumen Fund Global Fellows Program.

> Listening is not just having the patience
> to wait; it is also learning how to ask
> the questions themselves.

When she was starting out, Jacqueline never thought a simple career change would catapult her to the forefront of a new movement for economic justice. For some of us, it takes the better part of a lifetime to discover our life's work. Others form a clearer picture earlier in their careers. But one thing is certain: Life will bring us a myriad of experiences, and each of us will be drawn to a different gateway to start on our personal path. The only way we can know if we are going through the "right" doorway is by how it makes us feel inside. Feeling alive and inspired was—and is—essential to Jacqueline. She believes that listening is often the first leadership step we can take, both in our work with others and in our own hearts.

Perhaps Jacqueline's chance encounter with a Muslim Bohri woman best encapsulates what she has strived for all her life. In the virtually empty Chhatrapati Shivaji International Airport, in Mumbai, it seemed especially strange that a woman wearing a large cape and a head covering sat down right next to her, flashing a toothless smile. She clapped her hands together, turned to Jacqueline, and said, "I could see that you are deeply happy sitting there all alone, but you are not lonely. I could see that you are one of the happiest people, the ones who serve the world. You know, there are so many paths in a life. But the best are the ones where you are living the truth and searching for good and giving to others. Maybe that is what you are finding."

Jacqueline says that her experiences with the people she strives to help have been the most inspiring. They have remarkable endurance and resilience, she says, along with a capacity to dream of a better life. Early on in her career, some shortsighted naysayers had tried to dissuade her, dismissing her bold ideas as nothing more than pipe dreams. But something inside told her to put her convictions and talents to work, to take risks—and create change.

"It is not that good leaders are fearless," she once said. "But that they see possibility where others don't." Jacqueline Novogratz has surely earned her place among the pioneers of the possible.

Bibliography

"A Conversation with Architect Zaha Hadid," *Charlie Rose*, PBS, New York, NY, June 16, 2003.

"Amma.org: Embracing the World." http://www.amma.org.

Bair, Deirdre. *Anaïs Nin*. New York: Penguin, 1996.

Bair, Deirdre. *Simone de Beauvoir: A Biography*. New York: Touchstone, 1991.

Berg, Gertrude. *Molly and Me: The Memoirs of Gertrude Berg*. New York: McGraw Hill, 1961.

Born, Pete. "Leonard Lauder: The Visionary." *Women's Wear Daily*, December 9, 2010.

Brown, Louise. *Sex Slaves: The Trafficking of Women in Asia*. London: Virago Press, 2001.

Buckingham, Marcus. *Find Your Strongest Life—What the Happiest and Most Successful Women Do Differently*. Tennessee: Thomas Nelson, 2009.

Burkett, Elinor. *Golda*. New York: Harper Perennial, 2009.

Campbell, Joseph. *The Power of Myth*. New York: Anchor, 1991.

Ching, Yu-Ing. *Master of Love and Mercy: Cheng Yen*. Grass Valley, CA: Blue Dolphin Publishing, 1995.

Cintrón, Conchita. *Memoirs of a Bullfighter*. New York: Holt, Rinehart and Winston, 1968.

Cornell, Judith. *Amma, Healing the Heart of the World*. New York: William Morrow & Company, 2001.

De Mille, Agnes. *Dance to the Piper: Memoirs of the Ballet*. London: H. Hamilton, 1951.

Eaude, Michael. "Conchita Cintrón." *The Guardian*, February 20, 2009.

Ensler, Eve. *I Am an Emotional Creature: The Secret Life of Girls Around the World*. New York: Villard, 2011.

Firth Murray, Anne. *From Outrage to Courage: Women Taking Action for Health and Justice*. Monroe, ME: Common Courage Press, 2008.

"Forugh Farrokhzad." http://www.forughfarrokhzad.org

Freedman, Russel. *Martha Graham: A Dancer's Life*. New York: Clarion Books, 1998.

Glancey, Jonathan. "I Don't Do Nice." *The Guardian*, October 8, 2006.

Graham, Martha. "I Am a Dancer." *This I Believe*, Vol. 2, 1952.

Herrera, Hayden. *Frida: A Biography of Frida Kahlo*. New York: Harper Perennial, 2002.

Hersh, Phil. "One Hurdle After Another for Little Moroccan." *Chicago Tribune*, August 23, 1987.

Hildebrandt, Ziporah. *Marina Silva: Defending Rainforest Communities in Brazil*. New York: The Feminist Press at CUNY, 2001.

Hillman, Michael C. *A Lonely Woman: Forugh Farrokhzad and Her Poetry*. Washington, D.C.: Three Continents Press, 1987.

"Interview with Zaha Hadid," *Connect the World*, CNN, New York: NY, April 15, 2010.

Lauder, Estée. *Estée: A Success Story*. New York: Ballantine Books, 1985.

Maathai, Wangari. *Unbowed: A Memoir*. New York: Anchor, 2007.

Mam, Somaly. *The Road of Lost Innocence: The True Story of a Cambodian Heroine*. New York: Spiegel & Grau, 2009.

Mandela, Nelson. *Long Walk to Freedom*. New York: Little, Brown; 1994.

Martha Graham: Dance On Film. DVD. Directed by Nathan Kroll. New York: Criterion Collection, 2007.

Meir, Golda. *My Life*. New York: Dell Books, 1976.

Menchú Tum, Rigoberta, and Elisabeth Burgos-Debray. *I, Rigoberta Menchú: An Indian Woman in Guatemala*. London: Verso, 1984.

Milani, Farzaneh. *Veils and Words: The Emerging Voices of Iranian Women Writers*. London: I. B. Tauris & Co. Ltd., 1992.

Muschamp, Herbert. "Zaha Hadid's Urban Mothership." *The New York Times*, June 8, 2003.

Nicholson, Stuart. *Ella Fitzgerald: A Biography of the First Lady of Jazz*. Cambridge, MA: Da Capo Press, 1995.

Novogratz, Jacqueline. *The Blue Sweater: Bridging the Gap Between Rich and Poor in an Interconnected World*. New York: Rodale Books, 2009.

O'Neill, Mark. *Tzu Chi: Serving with Compassion*. Hoboken, NJ: Wiley, 2010.

Rahimieh, Nasrin, and Dominic Parviz Brookshaw, eds. *Forugh Farrokhzad, Poet of Modern Iran: Iconic Woman and Feminine Pioneer of Persian Poetry*. London: I. B. Tauris, 2010.

Rivera, Diego. *My Art, My Life: An Autobiography*. New York: Citadel Press, 1960.

Rumi, Jalal Al-Din. *Hush, Don't Say Anything to God: Passionate Poems of Rumi*. Translated by Shahram Shiva. Fremont, CA.: Jain Publishing Company, 1999.

Ryan, Raymund. "NYZ: New York Zaha." *The Architectural Review*, July 2006.

Samphier, Tony. "The NI Interview." *New Internationalist*, Issue 272, October 1995.

Seabrook, John. "The Abstractionist." *The New Yorker*, December 21 and 28, 2009.

Seymour-Jones, Carole. *A Dangerous Liaison*. London: Arrow, 2009.

Smith, Glenn D. *Something on My Own: Gertrude Berg and American Broadcasting, 1929–1956*. Syracuse, NY: Syracuse University Press, 2007.

Suzman, Helen. *In No Uncertain Terms: A South African Memoir*. New York: Alfred A. Knopf, 1993.

Taking Root: The Vision of Wangari Maathai. DVD. Directed by Merton, Lisa, and Alan Dater. Toronto: Mongrel Media, 2008.

Trebay, Guy. "Come to Mama." *The Village Voice*, July 21, 1998.

"Tzu Chi Foundation U.S.A." http://www.us.tzuchi.org

When the Mountains Tremble. Directed by Newton, Thomas Sigel, and Pamela Yates. DVD. New York: New Video Group, 1983.

Yoo-Hoo, Mrs. Goldberg. DVD. Directed by Aviva Kempner. Washington, D.C.: The Ciesla Foundation, 2010.

RAINFORESTS

SIMON & SCHUSTER

LONDON • SYDNEY • NEW YORK • TOKYO • SINGAPORE • TORONTO

First Published in 1991 by
Simon & Schuster Young Books
Wolsey House
Wolsey Road
Hemel Hempstead
Hertfordshire HP2 4SS
England

Copyright © 1991 by Simon & Schuster
Young Books

British Library Cataloguing in Publication Data

Knapp, Brian, 1946 –
Rainforests – (Caring for environments)
1. Tropical regions. Forests
I. Title   II. Series
333.75

ISBN 0-7500-0861-X

Printed and bound in Hong Kong

Author Dr. Brian Knapp
Art Director Duncan McCrae
Illustrator Mark Franklin
Designed and produced by
EARTHSCAPE EDITIONS,
86 Peppard Road,
Sonning Common, Reading,
Berkshire, RG4 9RP, UK

Picture credits

t=top b=bottom l=left r=right

*All photographs from the earthscape Editions
photographic library except the following:
Bruce Coleman 22t, Andrew Mendes 14t, 38t;
The Huthchison Library 29b, 35b, 36, 37; Kate
Simpson 23; ZEFA Front cover, 24t, 30t*

CONTENTS

1: WHAT ARE THE RAINFORESTS?

Rainforests – the forests that naturally clothe the land near to the Equator – are among the world's greatest treasures. They often reach the news because their future is of great concern, and they are frequently the subject of films. Yet despite this publicity, rainforests are some of the least well understood regions of the world.

People often call rainforests 'jungles'. This is a word that is easy to say, yet it is a name properly used only for one kind of rainforest: the kind where people have destroyed the original trees and where new saplings are springing up and competing for the light. A jungle

__Rainforests receive enough energy to support a multitude of creatures__. Here plants grow in great profusion even in the dim light of the forest floor.

__In undisturbed rainforests__ each tree jostles its neighbours in a never-ending fight to get enough sunlight.

is a forest recovering after a disaster such as logging, a place where there is little room for movement and relatively little variety in the wildlife. It is a long way from the more open rainforests that are undisturbed.

Rainforests are our most ancient natural lands. The effects of the world's great droughts or the ravages brought by the **Ice Ages** have all passed the rainforests by. Here the wildlife does not battle against the weather as it does in other parts of the world. The climate has remained steady, with plentiful warmth, sunshine and moisture, for millions of years.

The wet rainforests are ideal for creatures such as tree frogs.

Rainforests are no longer as widespread as in the past because the land has been used by people for other purposes. Rice fields are one of the better ways to use rainforest land: rice is the highest yielding of all cereal plants.

In the ancient rainforests nature has been able to produce a bewildering variety of species. This is one reason why, to the casual observer, the forest appears to be alive with resources. There are high trees of massive girth, good for timber, and for nuts or fruit. There is soil, far deeper than in any other part of the world, and there are animals of all shapes and sizes. This truly appears to be a bountiful land, and one that can supply all the needs of people who want to live there.

Yet in this land appearances are cruelly deceptive. It is a mistake to think of giant trees as a never-ending supply of timber; it is a mistake to think of the deep soils as suitable for crops; and it is a mistake to imagine that rainforest animals can successfully be replaced by herds of domestic animals. It is through such mistaken impressions that the rainforests have been subject to such savage attack. Too late have people learned that rainforests are fragile lands that must be treated more carefully than almost any other place on earth.

How people can survive in the rainforest, how they can benefit by its great resources, and how it can be preserved for future generations to enjoy, depends on understanding how the rainforest has evolved. This is described in the first part of this book. The second part of the book describes how people have tried to live in the rainforest and why they have often been defeated by it. The final part is about how we can look after the rainforest, especially in areas which are under great pressure from people.

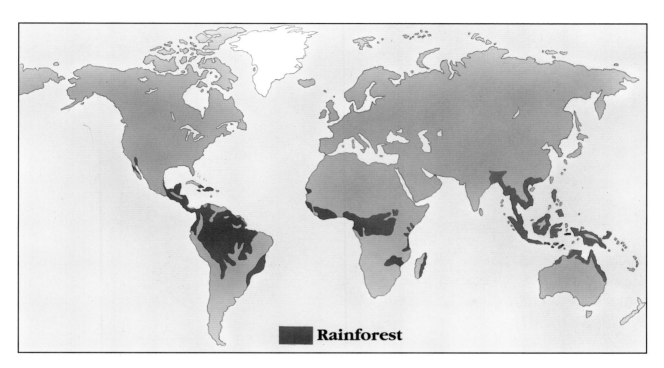

The natural extent of the world's tropical rainforests *is shown on this map. Many of these areas have now been cleared for farming or commercial tree-growing.*

In a natural rainforest many people live very isolated lives.
The main arteries of communication are often the rivers and the rainforest has mainly been exploited through its waterways. The highest concentrations of people are also found beside the rivers, although increasing numbers of roads are changing this traditional distribution and giving people access to previously remote places.

2: THE ENVIRONMENT

T o walk inside a rainforest is like walking in the tropical hot-house of a botanical garden: here you will find a constant temperature of about 30°C and enough moisture to give a sticky feel to the air. Much of the moisture, or **humidity**, is produced by the plants themselves, because the rainforest makes, at least in part, its own climate.

Rainforest weather

In the lands near the Equator weather forecasters would find little to do. The temperature hardly changes between day and night or from one month to the next. It is this evenness of the weather that is the secret to the rainforest's success.

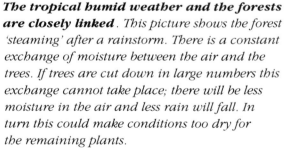

The tropical humid weather and the forests are closely linked. This picture shows the forest 'steaming' after a rainstorm. There is a constant exchange of moisture between the air and the trees. If trees are cut down in large numbers this exchange cannot take place; there will be less moisture in the air and less rain will fall. In turn this could make conditions too dry for the remaining plants.

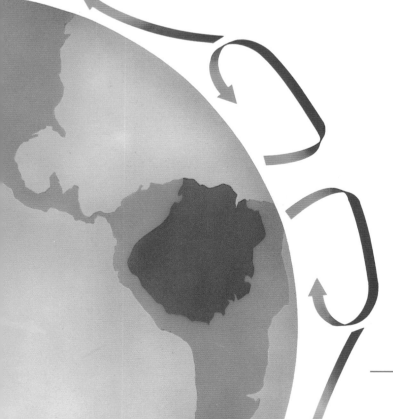

The tropics provide the heat engine that powers the whole global circulation of the atmosphere. Intense heating by the sun causes air to rise near the Equator. This zone of rising air is marked as 'low pressure' on weather maps. This is the place where thunderstorms are produced.

From this region air spreads out at high levels and sinks to the north and south where it creates the great deserts. Rainforests only exist below the region of rising air where rainfall is reliable.

Each day the sun rises quickly in the sky and heats the ground intensely. The warmed air then rises, drawing moisture from the surface and carrying it high into the sky where it cools and forms the water droplets that make clouds.

By lunchtime the sky is filled with clouds and by mid-afternoon it is pouring with torrential rain. In some parts of the world rainstorms occur very regularly each day for months on end. People can almost set their watches by them. In other places there is a little more variety, with a few months being less wet and more sunny than the others. But the key to a rainforest is that there should be enough rain so that the plants do not dry out, the pattern of rain ensuring a continuing supply of water for all the plants that grow.

Soil

When people walk through a rainforest their feet are cushioned by a layer of fallen leaves. They could hardly guess that below them lies one of the most unusual soils on earth, a place where rocks are constantly under attack from the warm, moist conditions.

All soil is formed by the destruction (or weathering) of rock. As the rainwater flows through the soil, so it acts like a diluted acid, slowly breaking down the rock and carrying away the soluble products of decay. In the rainforest this process has been going on unchecked for millions of years. In many places the soil is now many metres thick, tens of times thicker than it would be in other parts of the world.

The thick, old soil is mainly made of clay. It is a sticky material that will not easily wash away. But over the years rainwater has washed the **nutrients** away, leaving the soil quite infertile. In many soils, rotting has reached such a depth that there are no more rocks near the surface to be weathered and release supplies of nutrients for the plants. This situation has forced plants to adapt to survive. They are the world's best scavengers, capturing nutrients from the rain and dead plants to make up for what they cannot get from the soil.

This soil has been exposed in a road cutting. *The great thickness of weathering is exploited by using bulldozers to make cuttings. You can see the bulldozer scrape marks on the soil face. Few plant roots have penetrated the soil: there is nothing there for them to use.*

The land

In the hot humid soils beneath rainforests, the rocks are turned into clays and few stones ever find their way to river beds. Without this natural 'sandpaper' to help to scour the channels, rivers in rainforest lands have little erosive power and they mainly cut insignificant valleys. The landscape is only carved into deep valleys and hills near to mountains. As a result, the vast majority of the land is dominated by flat plains.

The only rocks that are not attacked by tropical weathering are called **quartzites**. They are made of a material that has the same kind of chemistry as glass. This material is almost immune to chemical weathering, and cannot readily be attacked by rivers because they do not have the stones to wear it away. As a result, quartzite rocks are responsible for some spectacular waterfalls.

The Kiteur Falls on the Potaro river in Guyana occur where an unusually tough band of rock resists the normal chemical attack of rainforest acids.

A surprise underfoot! This boulder has been taken from deep inside a cutting made by a bulldozer. It looks sound enough and most people would not risk dropping it near their bare feet. But when this boulder is dropped it proves to be so rotten that it simply smashes into tiny clay fragments.

Water streams down in front of the open door of this hut in the tropical rainforest. It is mid-afternoon, but the sky has turned dark and become obscured by the torrential downpour.

Living with the weather

The hot, humid conditions of the tropical rainforests are difficult for people. It is impossible to work hard for long periods without becoming very fatigued and risking collapse through **heat stroke**. The high humidity makes matters worse because the normal cooling effects of sweating are ineffective.

People in the tropical rainforests have traditionally worn little clothing, exposing as much skin as possible to any cooling breeze that might be available. Houses are designed to let air circulate as freely as possible. Shelters are used to keep dry in the rain, and possibly as protection against animals during the night. All buildings feature large openings (windows), and walls that have an air gap between the top and the roof.

Because there is a high risk of rainwater pouring over the floor of a house built on the ground, many people construct their homes on stilts. The space below the floor doubles up as a shelter for domestic animals at night.

3: FOREST WILDERNESS

You might think that plants and animals living in the rainforest find life much easier than in other areas of the world. After all there are no gales to blow down trees and no frosts to kill buds and shoots. There are not even any droughts which may force animals to migrate to other areas in search of food.

But this warm, rainy and very stable world is not as tranquil and easy as it seems. Indeed, survival in the rainforest is as difficult for its inhabitants as any other place on earth.

Finding a niche

The tropical rainforest is a naturally occurring collection of plants and animals that live in balance with the soils and climate. This **ecosystem** survives because every species is constantly battling for space in which to thrive and reproduce.

There is enough energy and moisture for a wide variety of species to find a **habitat** or niche that will suit their requirements. But a home is often suitable for more than one kind of inhabitant and there is often great competition between species.

The most prodigious plants are the rainforest trees. Reaching up to well over 45 metres from the ground, these trees capture much of the sun's energy in their dense canopy. Unlike trees in cooler regions, tropical trees can get their energy from a relatively small area of leaf. So they do not grow side branches, but instead race high into the air where they then spread out in the form of an umbrella.

Straight, tall trees leave lots of space for other kinds of species to grow among the giant trunks. Smaller trees and saplings, waiting their turn to be larger trees, occupy this open space. They cannot expect to get as much energy and their growth is slower. They often have large leaves to help to expose themselves to as much light as possible.

Even the dim light that filters through the tree canopy provides enough energy for a profusion of plants to grow. Here the stream banks are dominated by ferns, some of which grow to over 5 metres high.

Silent hosts

The giant trees provide much more than a dimly lit space between their trunks. They also provide a home and a structure on which plants can lean. High in the branches are plants that have no roots, but simply cling to their host tree using it as a convenient support. Bromeliads are among the most common of this type of plant, called an **epiphyte**. Their rosettes of leaves are specially shaped to funnel the rain down to the centre, and here nutrients are extracted directly from the water. It is a signal that plants do not necessarily need soil to get the food they need to survive, as we shall see later on.

Many plants are more demanding of their hosts; they are using them as way of surviving. Figs, of which there are innumerable species in the rainforest, wind up the trunks of large trees, using them to climb high into the forest canopy. At the same time they strangle the tree on which they are climbing, and often sink sucking rootlets into its bark to gain extra nutrients.

Figs provide many of the **lianas** of the forest, dangling branches that look like gnarled ropes from some monster cobweb.

In a rare break in a rainforest mountainside, a stream forges a narrow path. Notice how close the tree canopy has grown, and how the undergrowth plants near to the stream have grown up to take advantage of the extra light that reaches the ground

Bromeliads live in the moist space below the main canopy. Their rosette shape helps to focus rainwater to the centre, where it is stored until the plant can take out the nutrients. It is easy to see this work because bromeliads are common household plants.

One means of attracting pollinating insects near the ground is to provide large, bright flowers. Notice the broad leaves that are used to gather as much energy as possible.

How trees ward off their enemies

Most rainforest trees are evergreens. There are no harsh seasons to force them to shed their leaves and so leaves grow and are renewed throughout the year. But this continuous green canopy can easily become delicious food for a myriad of animals that live in the forests. So to combat them the tress have many survival strategies.

Some trees spread out near their base to give broad 'fins' which are called buttresses. They look as though they grow like this to support the massive tall trunks, but in fact they probably spread out to give all the roots the best possible chance of finding nutrients in the poor soil. The thin trunk growing between the buttresses is part of a fig tree.

One important means of survival is to attract large animals to their fruits. Many trees have luscious fruits that animals such as monkeys will eat whole. Then, as the monkeys move from tree to tree, they will scatter the indigestible fruit stones with their droppings. So not only has the animal benefited from the food, but the tree has gained from having its seeds dispersed to new growing sites.

Spreading seeds

All plants need to disperse their seeds because there are many hungry animals waiting to devour every leaf in sight. Fortunately for the trees, many insects – the most dangerous creatures for plant survival – have very specific eating habits. Each species often gets its food from the leaves of only one or two species.

If there were many trees of the same species growing side by side then a plague of insects might easily devour the trees one after another. But because each species of tree has scattered its seeds so well, plants are also widely scattered, making it much harder for insects to find each new plant to devour.

Trees do not just survive by chance, however. Many have tough bark and leaves to make them less easy to digest, while many others develop poisons in their leaves which make them dangerous for animals and insects to eat.

Self-sufficient trees

Many rainforest trees are so huge that it might seem inconceivable that they could survive in anything other than the most fertile of soils. And so it certainly seemed to many people who tried to cultivate the forest. But nothing is quite what it seems in a rainforest. For example, the giant trees often appear to prop themselves up with widely splayed roots called **buttresses**. Yet these buttresses are really not capable of holding the tree upright. What they are actually doing is making it possible for the roots to spread further in their search for food.

Trees in a rainforest have to be the most efficient plants of all, because the soil is not very fertile. The deeply weathered soils are, in fact, so old that all the rocks from which they are made weathered long ago. Millions of years of rainfall have washed away most of the nutrients and the soils are now **acid** and impoverished. Indeed, no trees could readily grow in such soils from scratch. But fortunately rainforest trees have an amazing network of roots that manage to scavenge all the nutrients. And, although they are the giants of the forest, their survival is helped by some of the most minute organisms of forest life.

An example of a tree being used as a prop by a climbing species. Like an ivy, this plant has small roots all along its stem which it uses to hold fast to the bark of its host.

Fungi hold the key

As the roots spread out in a network through the soil, they do not go downwards through the soil in search of minerals and water; there are, after all, no minerals and water is plentifully available. Instead, they grow just under the surface, sending up multitudes of tiny rootlets to the layer of rotting leaves scattered on the soil. Here a strange relationship occurs, whereby the root tips make use of microscopic fungi to digest the leaves and then transfer the nutrients to the roots.

This elegantly patterned butterfly is just one of thousands of tropical rainforest species. Each butterfly is a specialist, flying at its own special height and feeding from selected plants. It is the enormous variety of flowering plants that makes this possible.

In this way the trees manage to recapture the nutrients that were lost when they lost their leaves. And any tiny surplus that escapes can be made good as the roots soak up the minerals from each fresh rainstorm.

So it turns out that the trees are amazingly self-sufficient, that the soils are infertile, and that the forest survives only because there is an incredibly tight network of species all helping each other.

The roots of tropical rainforest trees stay near the surface where they can use the nutrients released by the decaying leaves. Here you can see the white rootlets literally on the soil surface.

Macaws are sociable, brightly coloured birds that are high canopy species, living and eating in the trees.

Their sociable habits have many advantages for survival. They operate a 'Neighbourhood Watch' scheme. With a combined total of several hundred eyes in a troop, they can readily spot a predator and send out a raucous squawking warning.

The many layers in this rainforest give an idea of the diversity of habitats in which creatures live.

The most dangerous place, and the one with least food, is the exposed forest floor, which is the reason why most animals are tree-dwellers.

Forest animals

Although the forest contains a wealth of animals, most people visiting a rainforest would see hardly any of them. Perhaps most conspicuous would be ants and beetles, some of gigantic proportions like the Goliath beetle shown on this page. Most of these are the decomposers of the rainforest ecosystem. They are clearing up the dead bodies and lost fruit and nuts that fall from the canopy above.

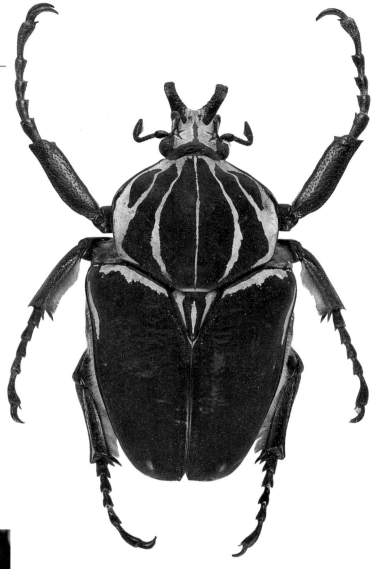

A Goliath beetle, shown here in life size, is one of the largest insects in the world, with a wingspan of up to 30 centimetres. One of the immense variety of insects that exists in a rainforest, each finding a special niche in which to survive, the Goliath beetle flies in the tree canopy where it eats fruit from the trees. Its larvae are wood-boring.

Monkeys are typical of the mammals that live in the middle branches of the canopy. They eat fruits in the trees as they move within their large territories and scatter the stones in their droppings.

A surprisingly large number of rainforest creatures live in the high branches. From monkeys and bats to macaws and butterflies, they are drawn to the high branches by the food growing on the trees. Because the trees have few lower branches there is relatively little to eat near the forest floor. By contrast there is nectar and fruit and fresh new leaves in abundance within the canopy. Equally important, it is also a relatively safe place, for the forest floor is home to carnivores like the leopard and tiger.

Jaguars are among the top carnivores in the *rainforest ecosystem. Their food consists of many of the forest mammals and, because of this, they have territories which may range over many tens of square kilometres.*

Many of the forest animals are very selective feeders. Their food may come from just one or two species of trees. And because the trees are so widely scattered, many animals have to forage far and wide to get enough to eat. This means that if we are to care for the forest animals, we must appreciate that they need large spaces to find their food. Small copses left to grow here and there amidst cleared land are not sufficient.

How a rainforest is renewed

Many rainforest trees attain a great age, but eventually each tree will die and crash to the ground. When this happens it may well cause other trees to fall as well, thereby opening up a space in the forest canopy.

The light which beams down to the ground in the resultant clearing triggers an enormous amount of life into rapid activity. For many years saplings have been staying almost **dormant**, waiting for such an opportunity. Now, with the extra energy from the direct rays of the sun, they spurt into growth, shooting upwards as fast as they can.

It does not take very many months for the once-open ground beneath a closed canopy to be transformed into a dense and often almost impenetrable jungle. Every species is making the most use of the sunlight while it lasts. But within a few years the strongest and most vigorous of the saplings will have won the race for the light, and they will send out an umbrella-shaped fan of branches whose leaves will start to create shade below.

The losers in the race often stop growing as the light is shaded out, and many others die away. The successful trees begin to close over the canopy and the ground is once more poorly lit and humid. The change, or succession, has taken its full course and the mature forest is re-established.

The conditions for renewal

The renewal of a forest takes place all the time. Animals are constantly eating fruits and then carrying the seeds away to be deposited on the forest floor. Beneath all mature trees there are saplings and seeds waiting to take over when the time comes. And they have to be quick, because the soil is so infertile that the nutrients released by the dead tree as it rots must be taken up by the new trees as they build their stems and leaves.

The race for survival can only be successfully fought in small clearings where the right conditions exist for new trees to spring up when their ancestors die. New rainforests colonize bare open ground very slowly because the conditions are not humid enough for the seeds and saplings to survive. Unlike weeds and grasses that can thrive in dry, open and sun-baked soil and which will rush in to colonize an area that has been cleared, a rainforest will retreat much more easily than it will advance.

The competition for space shows very clearly *where a river cuts through rainforest in the Congo, West Africa. Each tall trunk thrusts up to get part of the sunlight that reaches the canopy.*

6: USING THE TREES

The rainforest is truly a treasure trove for mankind. Rainforests contain the largest mass of tree material in the world. The trees are often hardwood and make fine building materials and furniture timber. The huge variety of species also means there is a tree for every purpose. The trees are therefore a great temptation to those who would make money from the forest.

What the trees can offer

Rainforest trees can provide people with all the necessities of a simple life. They can provide building materials that give homes and furniture; they provide fuelwood for cooking and heating; their nuts and berries provide

This boy from the South American rainforest has found a vantage point from which he can shoot at his quarry.
  Tribespeople can still find a good livelihood in the undisturbed areas of forest as hunter-gatherers.

Some of the more common fruits, nuts, herbs and spices found in supermarkets have their origins in the tropical rainforest. There are many other wild plants that could be cultivated.

Forest crop	Tree type	Origin
Banana	understorey tree	SE Asia
Brazil nuts	canopy tree	Brazil
Avocado	understorey tree	Guatemala
Passion fruit	climber	Brazil
Pineapple	bromeliad family	Paraguay
Lemon	understorey tree	Burma
Lime	understorey tree	Malaysia
Tapioca	swamp forest	Malaysia
Robusta coffee	understorey tree	West Africa
Cocoa	understorey tree	West Africa
Vanilla	orchid (climber)	SE Asia
Oil palm	understorey tree	West Africa
Cloves	understorey tree	New Guinea

food; and their sap provides materials that can be used for everything from sugar to cooking oil and glue. The trees also provide homes to a wide range of species that can be hunted for food.

The trees can also offer something that is less obvious. Because there are so many species, and because rainforests have existed for such enormous lengths of time, they now form the most valuable source of **genetic** material on earth. Scientists are only now beginning to understand how to make use of their properties to help provide medicines, and to feed the future world.

The hunter-gatherers

The people who have lived in the forest the longest are also the most knowledgeable about its ways. These peoples, often living as small groups or tribes within the main forests of Africa, South America and Southeast Asia, have learnt how trees can be used as food, as shelter, and even as medicine.

Some of these people do not cultivate the land at all. They are hunter-gatherers, relying on their ability to kill animals with bows and arrows or blowpipes, and their knowledge of where to find edible roots and seeds.

A selection of the fruits and nuts that can be readily obtained in our supermarkets and which come from rainforest trees.
You may be surprised at the variety.

Because there is no dry or cold season, the forests provide food all year round and they do not need to store or preserve foods.

The number of hunter-gatherers depends on the resources the forests can provide. If there are too many people relying on one area for their food, they will go hungry and may starve. For this reason hunter-gatherer tribes have always lived in small, widely spaced groups, each giving themselves enough territory for their survival.

Hunter-gatherer people are so dependent on the forest that they have had to learn how to live with it, how to make sure they do not over-harvest or destroy it. Much of this knowledge is passed on from generation to generation as rituals and religious ceremonies, thus ensuring that everyone is sensitive to their use of the forest.

Passion fruit

Banana

Brazil nuts

Lime

Harvesters

Tribes can harvest for their own use, but they can also harvest a surplus for sale. They can harvest not just nuts, like the Brazil nut, and fruits, like the banana, but also the sap of many trees, like the rubber tree. They can also crush the nuts of trees, like the palm, to make oil. Some trees even have a fragrant bark which can be cut and smoked to provide a pleasant aroma – a kind of incense.

Harvesting can be difficult, however, because each species of tree is widely scattered for its own protection. And while this is important for natural forest survival, it can be an inconvenience to the harvester. Not surprisingly, therefore, people have long sought to gather the most useful trees together to make the harvest more economical.

Just as in cooler regions there are orchards for collections of apple trees or orange groves for oranges, so in the tropical rainforests, many areas have been cut down and replaced with one or two species of tree. Each area of replanting is called a plantation.

The pictures above show the way the bark of the rubber tree can be scored to tap the sap. The white latex liquid is collected in a cup and then cured over a fire. Rubber collecting is done by smallholders and companies.

The picture to the right shows the way a rainforest has been replaced by **stands** of rubber trees on a hillslope. Rubber trees are shallow-rooted and do not protect the soil well. Widespread rubber plantations have been blamed for the increased flooding and loss of life that has recently occurred in countries such as Thailand.

Plantations are the oldest type of forest farming. The idea is to use the trees in their natural surroundings where they will grow well, but in patterns that will allow people to harvest the trees efficiently. Plantations are often managed by individual families (when the plantation makes up part of a smallholding) or they are organized into huge holdings managed by a company. These groupings of plantations are called estates, and were the way that former colonial countries organized the forests of their colonies. Because it is an effective system of farming, estates are still commonplace today – some government-controlled, others run by private companies.

Some improvements to protecting the soil can be made by growing crops on the ground beneath the trees. These are pineapples growing beneath rubber trees.

New for old

At first sight, the replacement of a rainforest with plantations of useful trees may seem to bring nothing but benefit. There is, after all, still a forest, and the tree cover remains intact. However, this is to miss the point about rainforest survival. There is good reason for the wide spacing of trees of similar species in a forest: it is to prevent the spread of disease or the ravages of pests. A plantation can be wiped out by an uncontrolled pest in a way that would never be possible in a natural forest.

This is an oil palm plantation. The rainforest has been replaced with trees which have been regularly spaced. Notice the way the ground is kept clear. This is very different from a natural forest. With trees planted together in this fashion they are very vulnerable to attacks by pests, and strong pesticides have to be used regularly.

Some of the more useful trees for people do not naturally make up the main tree canopy, but are weaker trees that naturally live in the understorey. Rubber trees are a common example. Rubber trees do not make a close canopy of leaves to keep out the effects of the torrential rainstorms and so they do not protect the soil as well as a natural forest. They do not have roots that can hold fast in a wet soil and they will readily fall over when planted in rows on a slope. So although people have gained the rubber resource, they have lost many of the valuable aspects of the forest.

Loggers

The loggers see the rainforest merely as a resource to be mined. They take away and they do not replace. Indeed even if they wanted to replace they could not: the rainforest is too complex an environment for simple replanting, and in any case people do not yet know how to raise many species in nurseries.

Loggers only cut down the trees that other people want. In general there is the largest demand for the biggest and tallest trees, and especially for those with the hardest wood. But these are the very trees that have taken longest to grow. A hardwood is hard because it grows slowly; it will not be replaced readily.

You can get some idea of the impact of logging by trying to picture a table with pencils standing end up all over it. Now imagine trying to take a pencil from the centre of the table out sideways without disturbing any of the others. Clearly it is impossible. In the past elephants were used to pull the logs from the forests. Elephants are extraordinarily careful and soft-footed animals and their impact on the forest was as small as it could be. Today, however, machines are used. They are faster, but much more destructive for the environment because their caterpillar wheels rip open the soil surface as they move along.

An area of forest that has been clear-cut.
The soil is left exposed and will erode with every storm. This is the most destructive form of logging.

The traditional way of taking logs out of a forest was to tie them to an elephant by a chain. The elephant would then pull the logs to the collecting point and then lift them into piles with its trunk. Logging by elephant was slow and this meant that there was a limit to the speed at which a forest could be exploited. Because elephants did not need roads, the forest remained relatively inaccessible and undisturbed.

The new way of taking logs out of a forest relies on bulldozers and trucks. Not only do the machines destroy the soil surface, but they also need more room than elephants to move about. Access roads are also vital if the logs are to be taken quickly to markets.

5: FROM FOREST TO FARM

It takes more than teamwork to clear an area of rainforest successfully. These women and children are preparing a 'garden' in the ashes of the forest, but they are unable to move the larger branches and stumps.

Two things have caused great concern for rainforest lands. The first has been a rapid growth of population, meaning more mouths to feed and a consequent need for more farmland. The second has been a change in the farmers. Now the majority are those who have been driven by pressures to the forests from elsewhere. They are not natives to the forest and they do not understand how quickly they can cause disaster.

Moving on

The forest can stand a certain amount of exploitation, but no more. If the land is cleared and used for farming for a short

Shifting cultivation can take place round a fixed village site. *Here the village clearing also shows the remains of stubborn stumps that the people cannot remove. The bare ground on the right is waterlogged and provides a new breeding place for parasites that does not exist in the native forest. At the same time the clearing has no protection against rain and water simply runs over the surface.*

The blackened branch of a tree shows that this land has been recently burned for farmland. The rice (the grass-like plants in this picture) is growing well, but so are the 'weeds'. When the land is abandoned the weeds will take over and rebuild the forest.

while and then abandoned, in time the trees will grow back in place. Forest peoples have cut and burned small areas – often known as 'gardens' – for countless generations. Because their tools are simple they cannot cut and remove the tree trunks. They simply set fire to a patch of forest and plant in among the burned and fallen branches and trunks.

For a few years the ashes from the forest will provide the nutrients that domesticated plants need. Maize, 'dry' rice (that does not need flooded land) and many vegetables will grow well enough under these conditions. But as soon as this temporary supply is exhausted the yields will fall and the

people will have to abandon the worn-out land and clear another area.

This practice is called shifting cultivation. Using shifting cultivation, a small tribe will need a large area to live on. But as populations grow and more people try to get food from the land they will be forced to replant before the land has recovered. Then, not only do they get poor harvests, but the forest never gets a chance to recover.

Paddy farming

The swampy lands near to rivers may seem best avoided, but it is where the oldest form of farming started – rice growing.

'Wet' rice, or paddy rice, is a curious cereal because, unlike all the other major cereals of the world, it thrives on water. Indeed, it cannot live unless the land is flooded while it is growing.

For thousands of years people have cultivated rice in fields that have been reclaimed from riverside swamp. And over the years people have learned how to manage this system well.

Each field is surrounded by a wall that keeps the water in, and each is connected by a system of feeder canals which admits fresh water from rivers. In addition, an equally vital system of drains lets stale water out of the fields before it stagnates.

Paddy farming uses the land intensively. As a result there is little room for forest trees, except the productive ones such as bananas or palms.

Even smallholders can often hire machinery to help them with the more tiring tasks of paddy farming. Here a special plough turns over the muddy soil after the fields have been drained. The white 'sheets' hanging on the line in the background are mats of raw rubber that have been collected from nearby trees.

This type of farming – called paddy farming – has been successful for so long because it uses the land in a sensible way. Rice has a higher yield than any other cereal. This means that large numbers of people can be sustained on relatively small areas.

Paddy farming traditionally used the land near to rivers because it is rich in nutrients drained from the rest of the rainforest.

Traditional wet rice cultivation is not a severe burden on the land, but uses nutrients that have been naturally fed to the fields. Rice farmers have many generations of experience to guide them in how to manage their land. And unlike the people who make gardens in the forest, the paddy farmers never need to move to new sites because they receive a constant supply of nutrients from the rivers.

As soon as the fields have been ploughed *they are flooded and rice seedlings are planted. For most people this is a back-breaking job.*

As the rice grows *this smallholder hoes between the lines of rice to prevent weeds from growing. Notice the wall separating the fields and how one section of it has been broken down to allow water to flow from one field to the other.*

The problem that many peasants face is that
they have no knowledge of the soil or the effects of
rainfall on bare soil. They are too poor to afford
fertilizers and so must adopt the tribal ways such
as burning the forest to clear it and release the
nutrients stored in the trees; yet they do not have
the tribal experience. Governments give peasants
fixed areas of land which they are forced to
overuse, whereas the tribespeople move from area
to area as the soil becomes exhausted.

Newcomers to farming

There are many newcomers to the
forest who are unskilled in the techniques
needed to deal with it and through their
ignorance they have caused widespread
devastation.

Each continent has its own story to
tell. In Indonesia they may have migrated
from the densely populated paddy lands
of Java to the almost unpopulated
rainforest of Sulawesi. In Brazil they
may have come from the drought-ridden
northeast to the rainforests of the states
of Amazonas and Rondonia.

But wherever they have come from,
it is almost certain that the stories they
have heard will have been false. There
is a saying that a little knowledge is a
dangerous thing. Nowhere is this more
apt than in the fragile rainforests. The
knowledge that the newcomers have
is often no more than hearsay. They
choose to believe that the land is dark,
rich and fertile. It is not.

To run a farm needs more than
back-breaking toil. It needs seed, proper
techniques and a market to which to sell.
The peasants are often too poor to have
any of these. Many arrive, work the land
without success and then leave. But there
are always thousands more to follow,
willing to chance their luck, not knowing
how heavily the odds are stacked against
their success. They, and the cattle
ranchers who destroy forests and plant
grass, are the farmers who threaten
the rainforest the most.

This is typical of land that has been cultivated *without knowledge. The long thin lines of crops can do little to prevent soil erosion. Before long this sloping field will be stricken with deep gullies that will make the land unworkable.*

While peasants tend their small plots, some large companies have bought vast areas of rainforest *to turn into cattle ranches, seeing the cheap land as a way of making money.*

These companies should have the resources to know better. Instead they show surprising ignorance of the capabilities of the land. Despite the use of the latest machines and doses of fertilizers, grasses have grown poorly, cattle have caught diseases, and no-one has made any money. Large tracts have been abandoned and the rains have eroded the soils. Both people and the environment have lost.

6: OUTSIDERS

Outsiders are people who do not naturally live and work in the rainforests. They are people who do not value the land except as a resource to be mined or used in some other way.

For many poor peasants their dream is to find an outcrop of gold ore that will make them wealthy and allow their families to lead a better life. For the large corporation and government department the goal is to make use of the wide range of minerals that lie buried. Gold may be one of these, but as much wealth can be made from iron, aluminium, tin and copper – all plentiful under the rainforest soils.

The search for gold

People have always sought to find gold and make their fortunes. The people who now search in the South American rainforests, for example, have the same objectives as the people who made their fortunes in California or in Alaska's Klondyke during the nineteenth century.

There are probably hundreds of thousands of people mining in the rainforests. Even so, their impact might not be important but for two things. First, their arrival opens up the forest. Roads are built to bring services to them

and soon towns develop. With towns come more permanent settlers and the end to the natural forest. Second, and just as important, the techniques the miners use are primitive and harmful to the environment. In particular the miners use mercury to extract gold from the rock. A small digging can pollute and poison a stream for tens of kilometres downstream.

Untapped wealth

Peasants like the Brazilian 'galimperos' do much damage, but their efforts are puny compared with the damage that can be done by large commercial organizations using open-cast mining methods.

Open-cast happens like this. First a large area – often many hundreds of square kilometres – is cleared by burning and bulldozer. Then the soil is pushed to one side. Below the soil the rotted rock contains perhaps iron, aluminium or copper. Even a rock with just one or two percent of copper is a rich find, so just imagine how much rock has to be bulldozed and put through smelting machines to yield a million tonnes of metal. And the companies are after many millions of tonnes a year in order to pay back the cost of the equipment and make a profit.

The people working in this mine are called galimperos. They are the peasant miners of Brazil. This is the most famous, and most productive mine in Brazil, called Serra Pelada. Fortunes have been made here, though few will be made in the future because the hole is too deep and the sides are constantly collapsing. The fact that, despite the dangers, people keep working here is an example of how desperately poor these people are. Given this degree of poverty, these people cannot be expected to show any real degree of care for their environment.

Miners disturb vast amounts of soil and rock, then they wash it to reveal the gold. The washings return to the rivers where they make the water muddy and unsuitable for many kinds of wildlife. In the mining process many dangerous heavy metals are released into the water. As a result mercury poisoning is now commonplace amongst the people who drink river water near to mines. The metals also build up in the fish and other river creatures. This not only kills the animals but helps to poison people when the animals are eaten.

Smelting

Smelting means heating rock until the metal runs free and can be tapped off. To make the heat either coal, oil, gas or charcoal have to be used. In the rainforests, coal, oil and gas supplies are not easy to get. But all around lie forests which can be cut down and made into charcoal.

Smelting means that the miners not only clear the forest for the ore, but far worse, they clear enormous areas of extra land to fuel the hungry furnaces. In fact the forests are destroyed so quickly by this means that there would be little chance of keeping pace by replanting even if large scale efforts were made – and they have not. As a result the search for minerals represents one of the forest's more serious dangers.

Power to the people

One reason why people in developing countries are poor is because many of them have to spend so much of their money paying for imported oil. Governments in such countries see any large river as a way

Most rainforests occur on gently sloping land. *When dams are built to supply hydro-electric power the water stored behind them often reaches for thousands of square kilometres.*
When trees are even partially drowned they soon die.

of generating hydro-electricity. But this means that many rainforests are in danger from flooding. No-one will use the timber, the trees will simply be drowned.

Countries have set about dam building projects with gusto. The only problem is that many countries now have more electricity than they know what to do

This is a small area of the land that was used for open-cast tin mining and then abandoned.

All of the species that have been planted around the patio by this swimming pool grow naturally in the rainforest. Here they have been selected for their decorative properties.

This part of the Malaysian coast has been changed to make room for a hotel complex. Some mature palms have been left, and others have been planted. Grass now grows between the trees. This gives the tourists a comfortable place to sit and admire the sun as it shimmers over the sea.

with. The forests have often been destroyed for no purpose. Building these large schemes is the wrong way to help the majority of the people.

Making a holiday paradise

The climate that gives the warmth and rain to make a tropical rainforest can also provide the ideal place for a tourist holiday. Many areas whose natural vegetation is rainforest are described in the holiday brochures as 'Tropical Paradise'.

But to make the coastal rainforest into an ideal tourist resort requires much effort on the part of the hotel trade. First the forest has to be cleared to make room for hotels, golf courses, roads and airports. Most rainforest trees look very straggly when they are exposed by forest clearance. Many are replaced by palms transported from inland plantations. Then, when all this has been done, and the land manicured and made to look nice, the tourists will arrive, but the rainforest will have gone.

7: IS THERE A FUTURE?

We can only care for our environments if we understand the way they work, *and* appreciate the reasons they are threatened. For example, we cannot just try to save the trees in a rainforest without worrying about the insects because every living thing is part of a balanced cycle, or ecosystem. Soil, plants and animals are all dependent on each other.

We also have to understand that the way a rainforest works is unique. It cannot be managed in the way we might manage, say, a temperate woodland. A rainforest survives because its species are widely scattered. In turn this means that, if we want to preserve the rainforest, we cannot simply preserve scattered clumps wherever it is convenient because then many of the species will be missing, and others will have too little room to scatter their seeds. Clearly the only way to preserve the natural forest is in very large tracts of undisturbed land. Even a road and cleared verges can be too much disturbance if it makes the land more accessible to people and drives wildlife away.

Matching wealth to care

People have to have a reason to care. The hunter-gatherers of the rainforests must care because their way of life – their survival – depends on the rainforest. People in the developed world with ample to eat can afford to care because they do not depend on the rainforest for their survival. In between lie a range of people each with their differing motives.

Hardwoods can be carved into beautiful furniture. Rainforests will continue to be destroyed unless plantations of hardwoods are established.

You might not recognize this piece of a rainforest because it has been turned into a bowl. Beautiful though the bowl might be, if there is too much exploitation of the forest the only place the rainforest will survive in the future will be in people's houses!

Many people simply want to make a better life for themselves. They would argue that they cannot afford to care because they are poor and the only way they can survive is through farming land. Governments sometimes say that it is their responsibility to improve the wealth of their people. This is why they allow logging, burning and mining.

Everyone has a right to a decent way of life. But the people who destroy the forest are not improving their lives in the long run, because in general their farms fail in the poor soil and the trees disappear, leaving them with no more forest to log. So it is important to make sure that fewer and fewer people need to destroy the forest. This is best done by making it easier for people to make their living in other ways.

No rainforest creatures will be safe while people throughout the world still pay high prices for the skins and furs of wild creatures.

Industry not only uses large areas of forest, but it is often a cause of pollution in the air and in rivers. Caring for the rainforest involves keeping tight controls on industry.

Giving the forest a wealth

Rainforests have wealth. At the moment it is the value of the hardwood trees for window frames and furniture. It is the soil for growing crops, and it is the rock for

Beauty is in the eye of the beholder. *As more and more people begin to understand the wonders of a rainforest – often by seeing nature films on television – the more they will see the rainforest as a place of beauty and want to visit it. This picture shows the kind of landscape more people can enjoy.*

producing metal ore. But this could change. There are two ways to do this. One is to stop buying forest products. For example, if people did not buy tropical hardwoods then there would be no demand and fewer trees would be cut. But a better way is to give the forest more value when left alone than when used for logs and farms.

One way of caring for the rainforest and preserving logging jobs is to set aside plantations of hardwoods that can be replanted time after time. It therefore makes sense to buy hardwoods only from places with a replanting programme.

Another way is to bring tourism to rainforests. Tourists spend considerable amounts of money. If a rainforest tourist industry develops in a way that makes people sensitive to the land, then it will be more profitable for local peoples to preserve the forest than to cut it down.

Seeing the dangers

People have to be made to see the danger to themselves of destroying the forests. This happened recently in Thailand where, in just twenty years, the country's forests were reduced from 80% of the land to under 20%.

As more and more trees were cut down and replaced with rubber trees or other crops, so the amount of water that could be stored in the soil became smaller. Finally, with each rainstorm there were devastating floods that killed many people. This helped the people to understand the damage they had caused, and the government was then able to put a ban on further logging with the consent of the people.

Simple facilities make all the difference to tourism. *It is not necessary to build huge hotels amidst the forest. This floating restaurant is a good example of simple, effective design that does little harm.*

Making National Parks

National Parks are used in many countries of the world to preserve areas as wilderness. They are only effective if they are big enough to allow the natural world to thrive.

It is easiest to set up National Parks before land comes under pressure. For example, many National Parks were set up in the western USA in the last century when there was relatively little pressure on the land. Now is also the time to set up National Parks in the naturally remote areas of the rainforests of the world. Venezuela has already set a lead in this, and some other countries have begun to follow. But a National Park need not be a place where all people are kept out, for the hunter-gatherer tribes will not damage the forests. People living in National Parks who depend on the forest for survival are the best guardians of the forest's future, for they will help stop people from logging and mining

Tin mining has left a terribly scarred landscape*. The remains of the rainforest will soon be destroyed as the cliff collapses. In trying to reclaim the tin mining land a golf course has been built to attract tourists. The ground has therefore been replanted to grass.*

illegally. This, too, has been the new Venezuelan policy.

In the end the way to preserve the forests is to take the pressure away. This means finding other jobs for the poorer people. It is not an easy task, yet until it is done the rainforests will continue to be under threat. Caring for the rainforest environment is a matter of understanding.

GLOSSARY

acid soil

a soil that has few plant nutrients in it and which is too poor for soil organisms to thrive. Most plants that live on acid soils have to be very efficient at recycling their own nutrients

buttresses

the name given to the fin-like structures that radiate out from the lower trunks of some rainforest trees. They are part of the root system and do little to hold the tree upright

dormant

a state where a plant or seed appears not to grow at all, but simply remains 'resting' and waiting for an opportunity to grow when conditions become right

ecosystem

a balanced arrangement of plants, animals, soil and climate. An ecosystem is a stable unit, with the decay of dead organisms providing the food for those that are growing

epiphyte

a plant that can grow without any roots, simply making use of the nutrients that wash in with the rainwater. Epiphytes grow especially well in places where rain is common, such as a tropical rainforest

habitat

the combination of environmental conditions that provide a suitable living environment for a species. An animal may find tree tops a good habitat; the habitat for a plant will include satisfactory soil and shade conditions

heat stroke

an illness brought on by overworking the heart in conditions of high humidity and temperature

humidity

the amount of water vapour in the air. Very humid conditions frequently occur in rainforests, allowing many creatures such as epiphytes to survive without any roots

Ice Age

a period when the world's ice sheets expanded greatly. As a result many areas lost their natural vegetation and it has only just recovered. An Ice Age only made the tropical rainforest belt narrower, it did not change its character

lianas

thick stems and roots that seem to hang from trees in some types of rainforest. Many lianas are stems of climbers such as figs

nutrients

the essential foodstuffs that living things require to grow. Nutrients for plants are released when dead tissue is decomposed. Calcium, nitrogen and phosphorus are examples of common plant nutrients

quartzite

a rock made entirely from quartz. Quartz is commonly found on the beach as sand grains. It is a very stable mineral and will not usually weather

stand

the name given to a group of trees of the same species that occur together within a forest

INDEX

access to forests 11, 29
acid soils 19, 44
animals 18
ashes from trees 30

bromeliads 17
buildings, traditional 15
burning forests 31, 34
buttress roots 18, 19, 44

canals 32
canopy 8, 16, 17, 21, 23
carnivore 21
cattle ranchers 34-35
charcoal 38
clay soil 13,14
clear-cut forest 28
clearing in forests 22
climate 9
climbing species 19
clothing 15
clouds 13
colonization 23
communications 11
copper ore 37
crops 10

dam building 38
decomposers 21
dormant 22, 44

ecosystem 17, 22, 40, 44
elephant 29
energy 8, 16
epiphytes 17, 44
estate farm 27
evergreen trees 18

farming 41
ferns 16
fertilizers 35
flooding 26, 38, 42
forest wealth 42
fragile lands 10
fuelwood 24, 38
fungi 19

furnaces 38
furniture 24

galimperos 37
genetic materials 25, 44
gold 36
ground heating 13

habitat 16, 44
hardwood trees 28, 40
heat stroke 15
humidity 12, 15, 44
hunter-gatherers 25, 40

Ice Age 9, 44
industry 41
iron ore 37

jaguar 21, 22
jungle 8, 22

landscape 14
lianas 17, 44
loggers 28, 41, 42
low pressure 12

markets for logs 29
medicinal plants 25
mercury poisoning 37
mining 41
monkeys 18

National Parks 43
nutrients 13, 19, 33, 44

oil from trees 26-7
oil palm 24
open-cast mining 36-8

paddy farming 32
palm trees 39
peasants 36
plantation 26
poisons in leaves 18

pollution 37
poverty 37
predator 20
preservation of forest 40
protecting soil 27

quartzites 14, 44

rainforest distribution 11
rainstorm 12, 15
replanting 42
resources 10
rice 10, 32
roads 11, 36
roots 20, 25, 28
rubber 26, 28, 32

scavengers 19
scouring of channels 14
seeds transport 23, 25
Serra Pelada, Brazil 37
shifting cultivation 31
smallholding 27, 32
smelting 38
soil 10, 13
species 10, 16, 18, 25
stands of trees 26, 44

temperature 12
thunderstorms 12
timber 10
tin 38, 43
tourism 39
tree-dwelling animals 20
trees 16
tribal experience 24, 25, 26, 34

vanilla 24

waterfalls 14
weather 12
weathering 13, 14
wilderness 16
wildlife 41
working 15